FOTO BOOTH

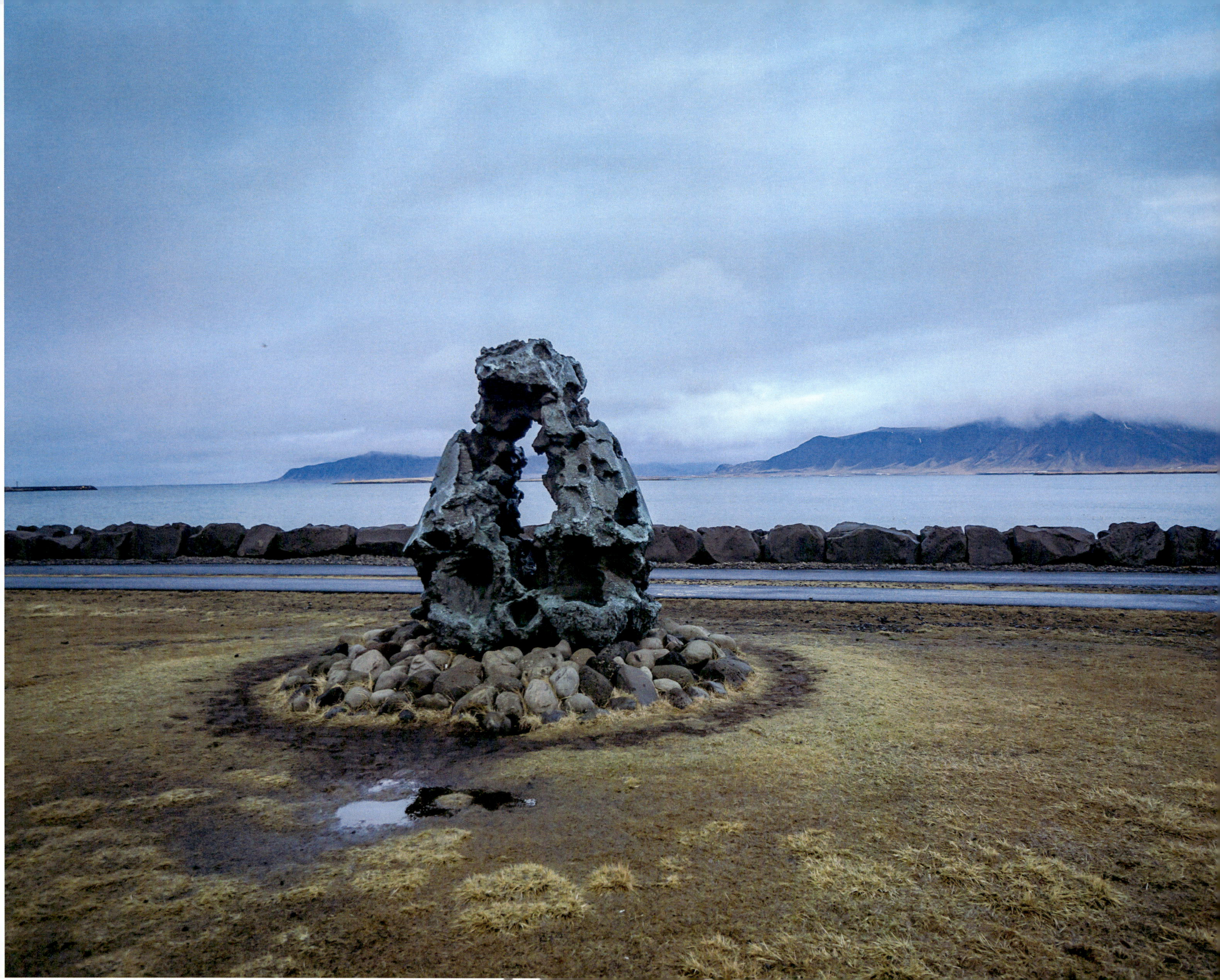

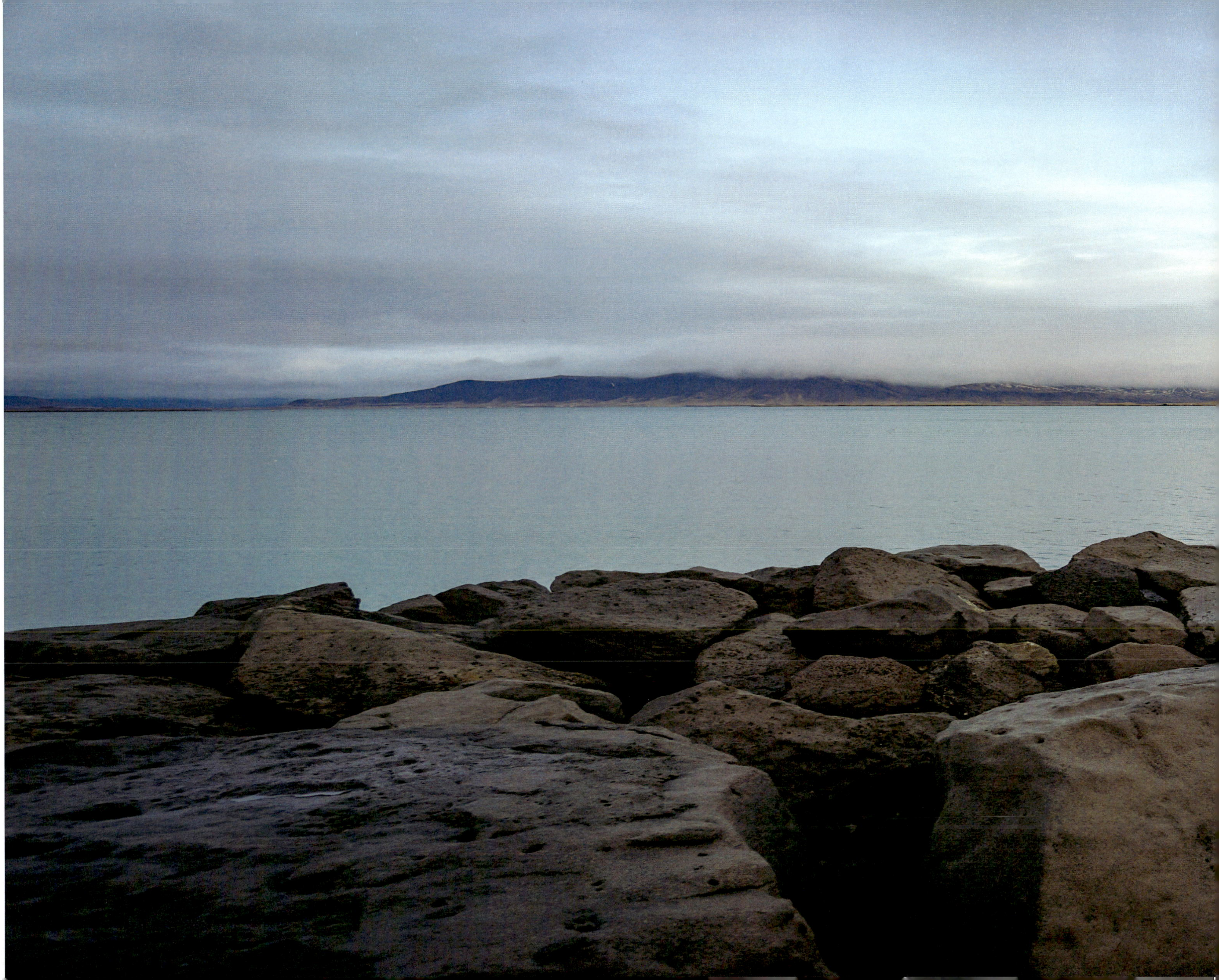

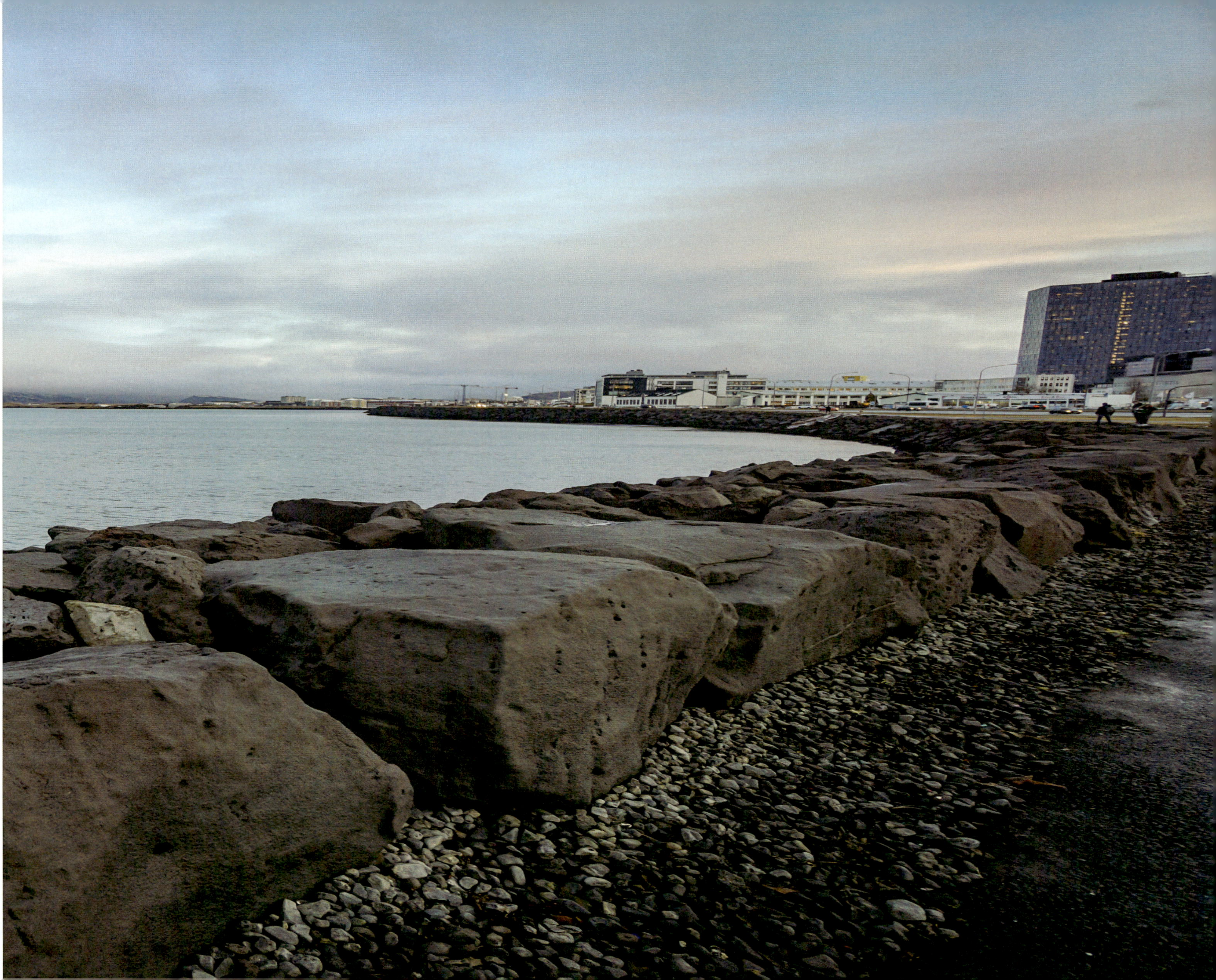

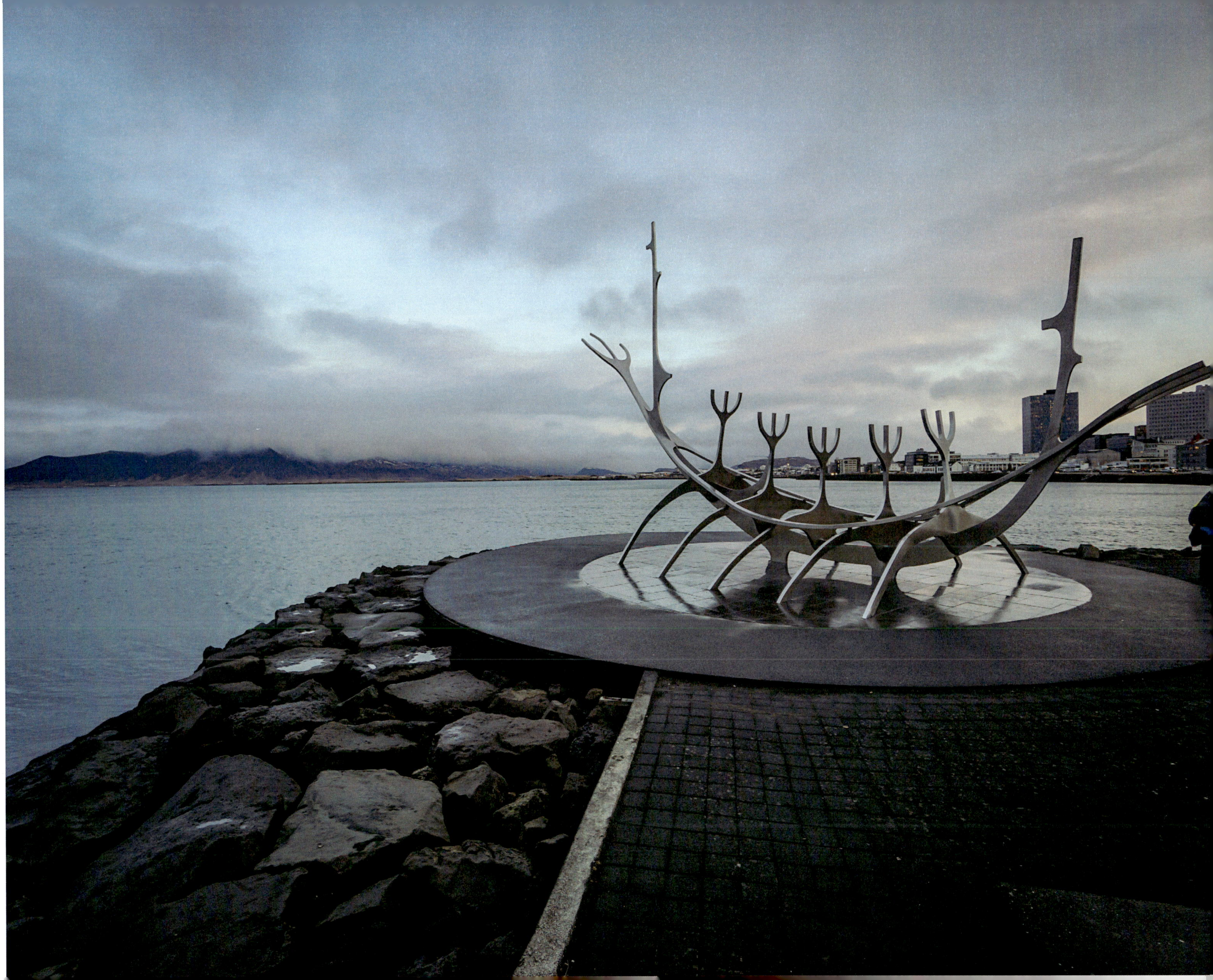

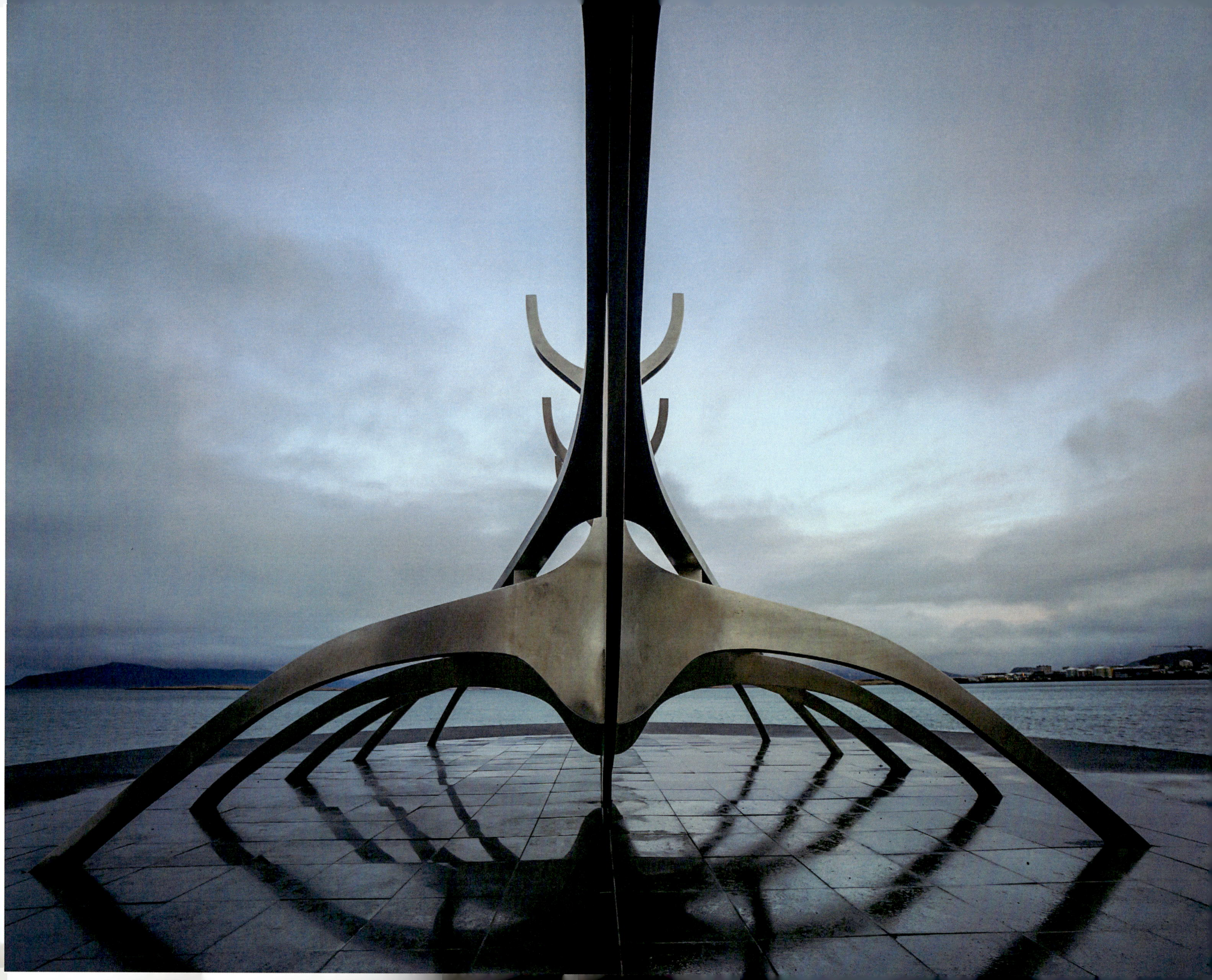

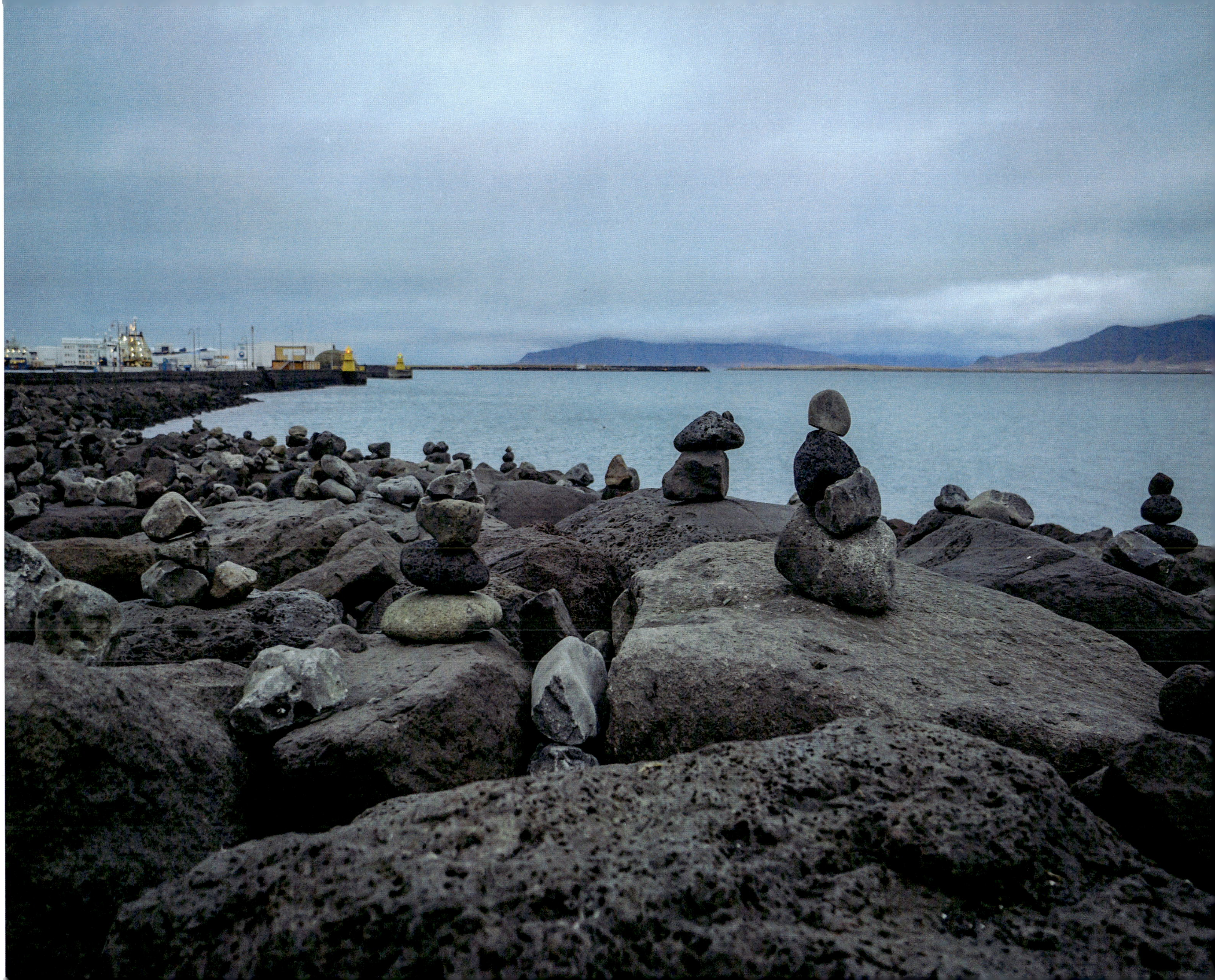

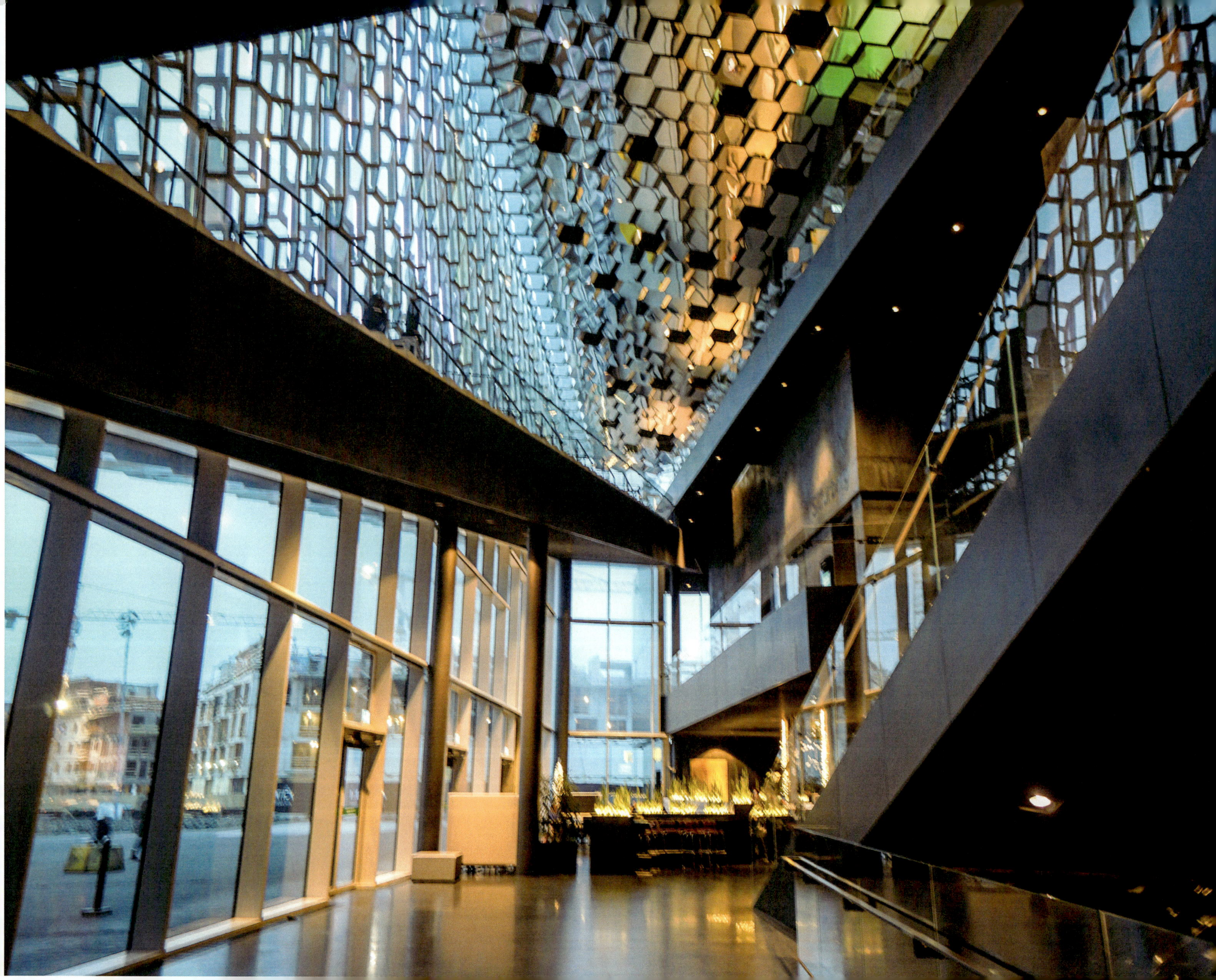

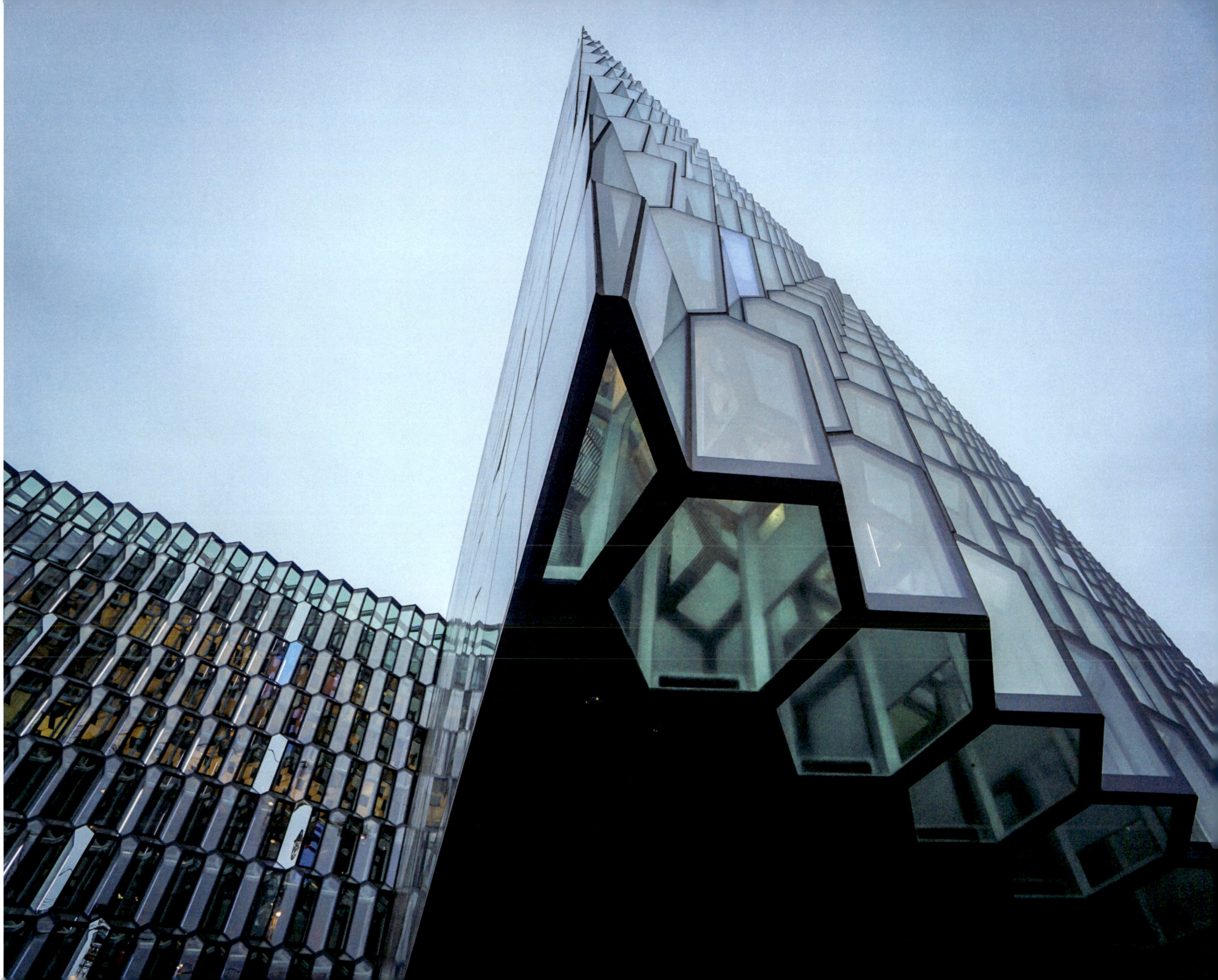

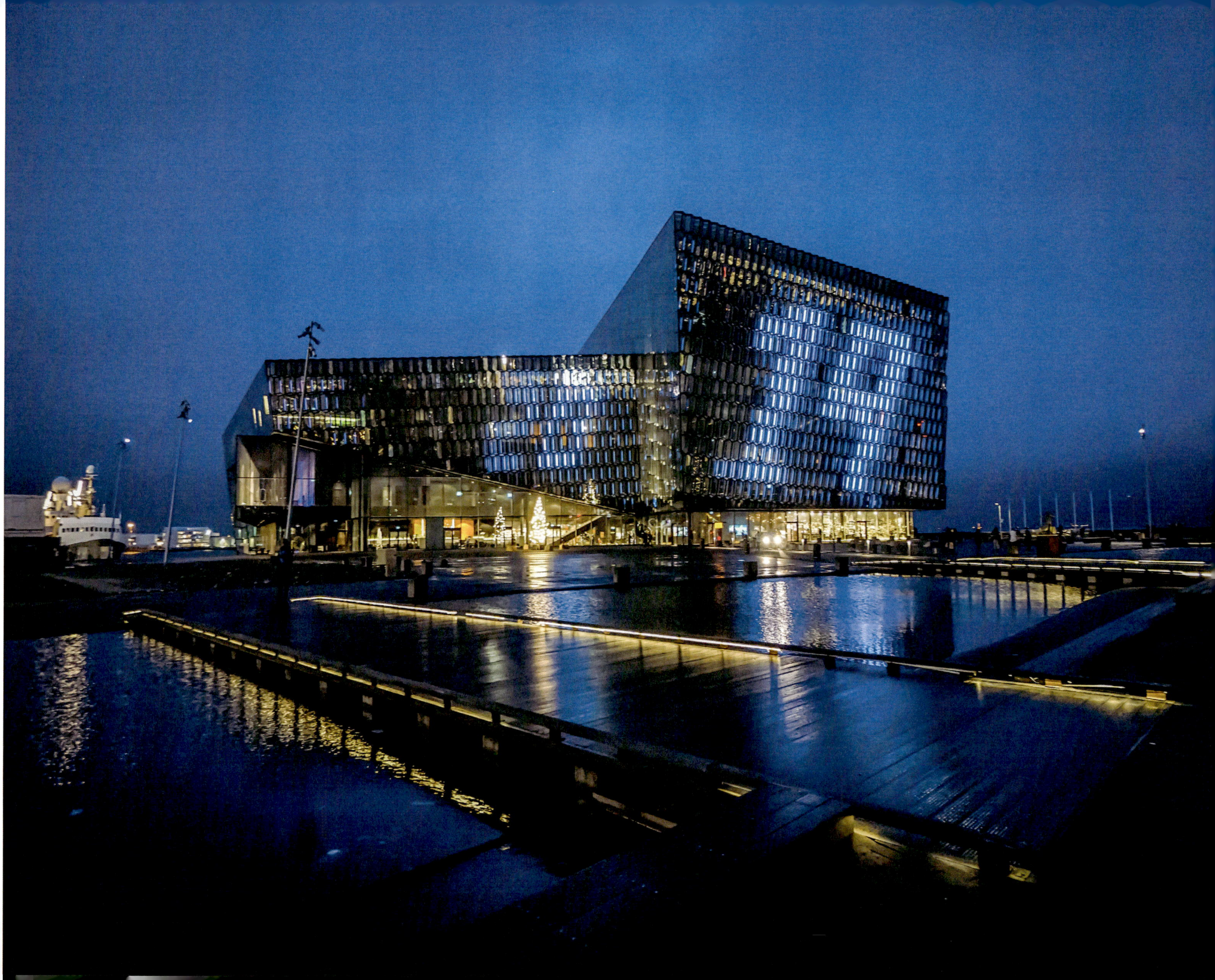

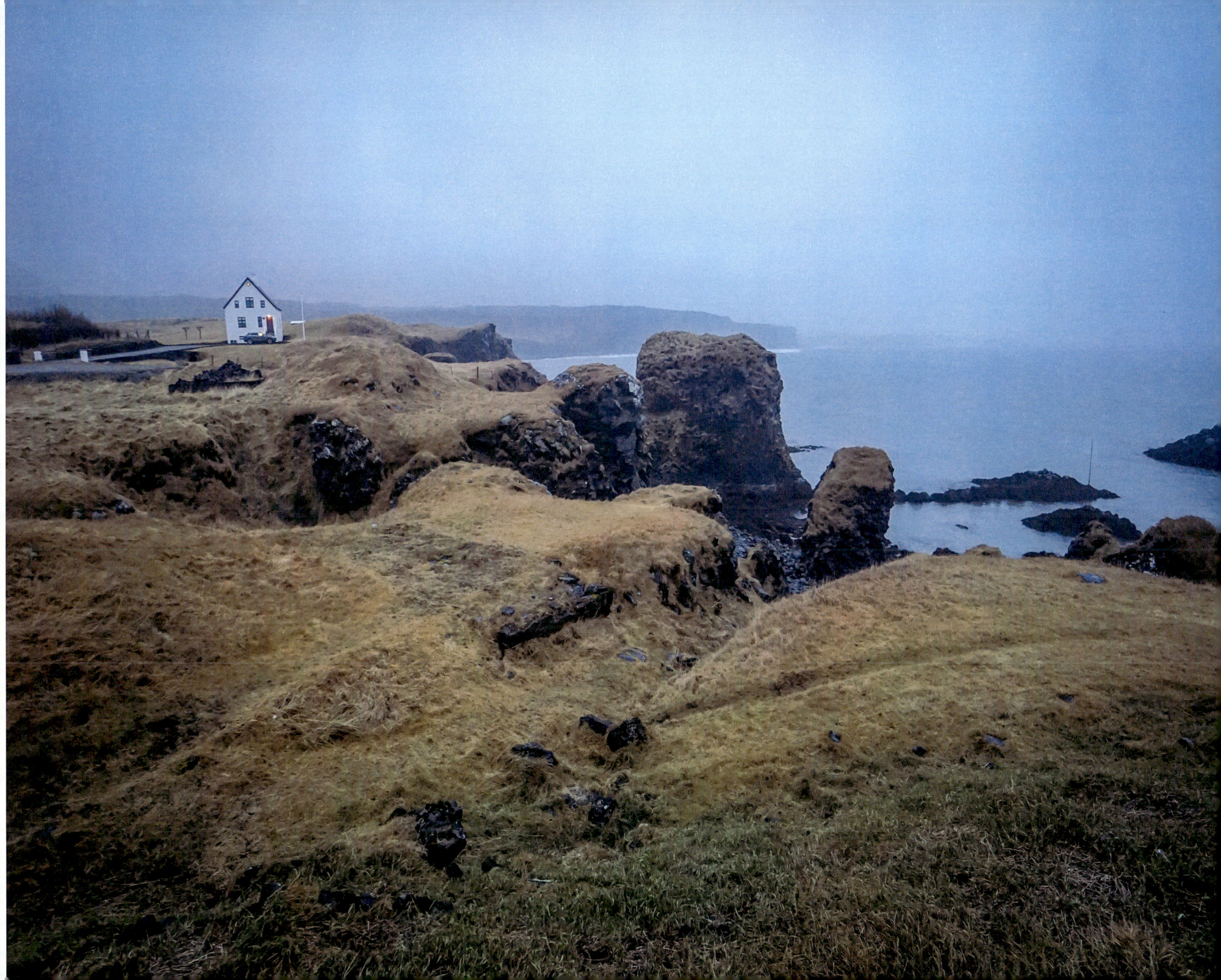

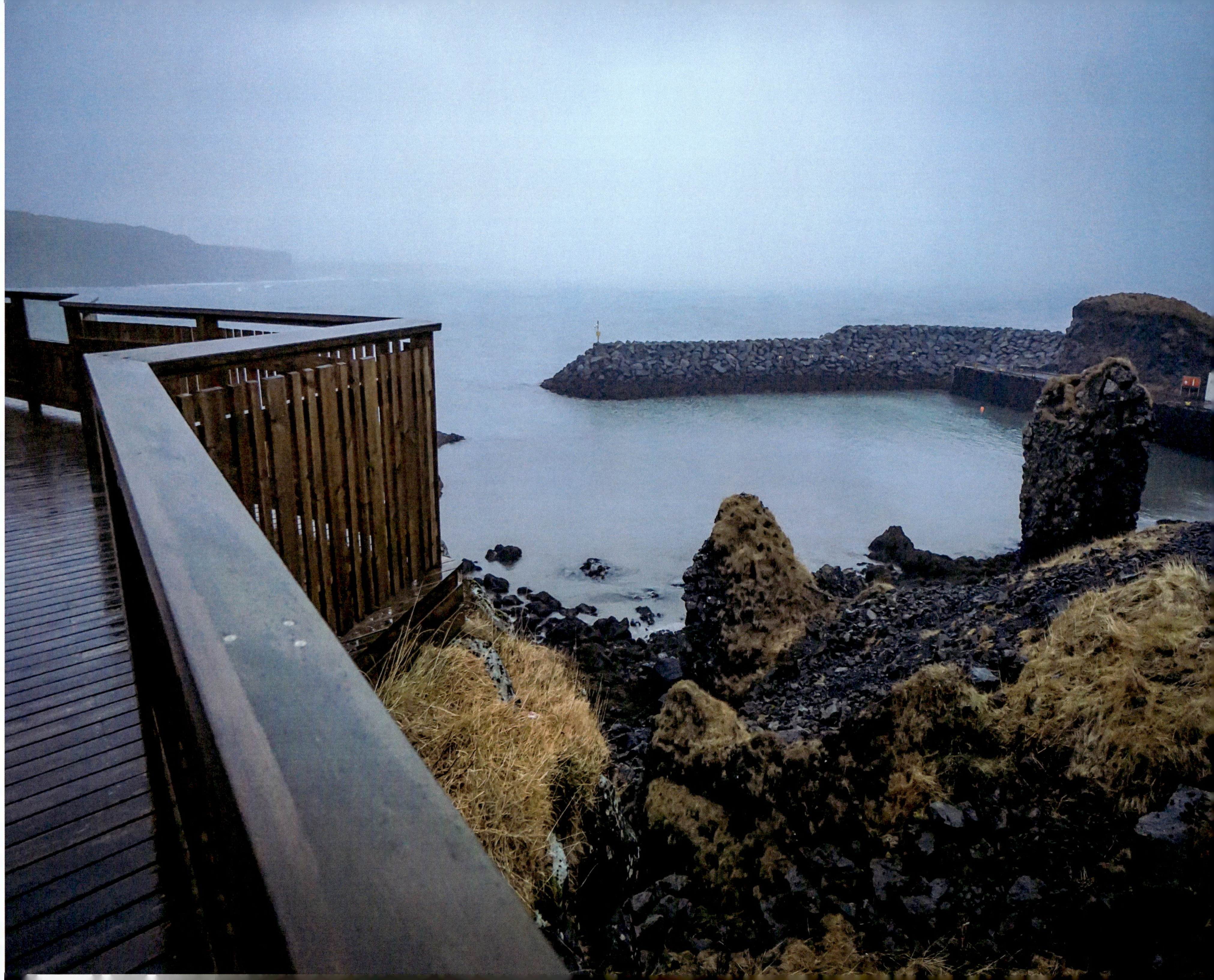

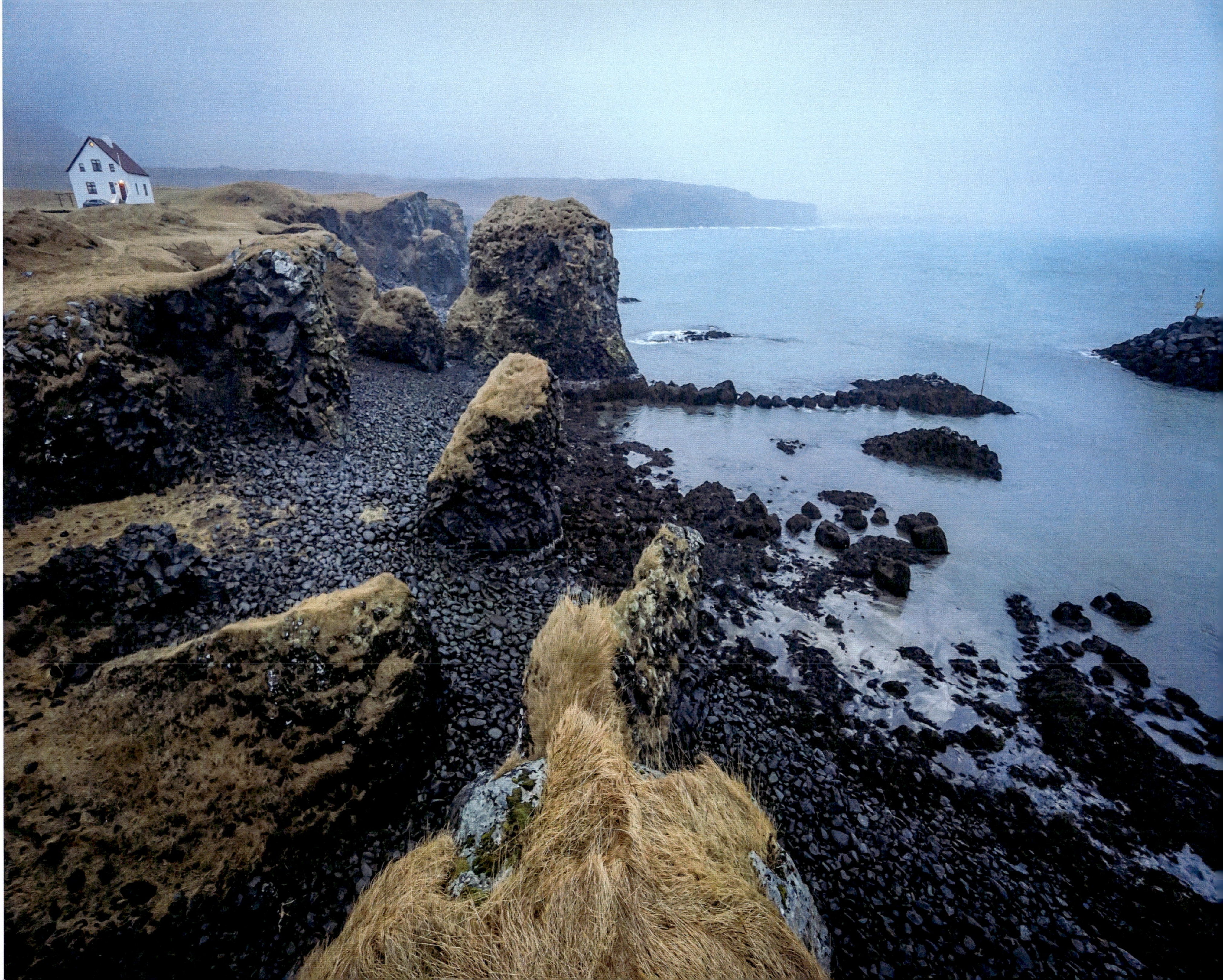

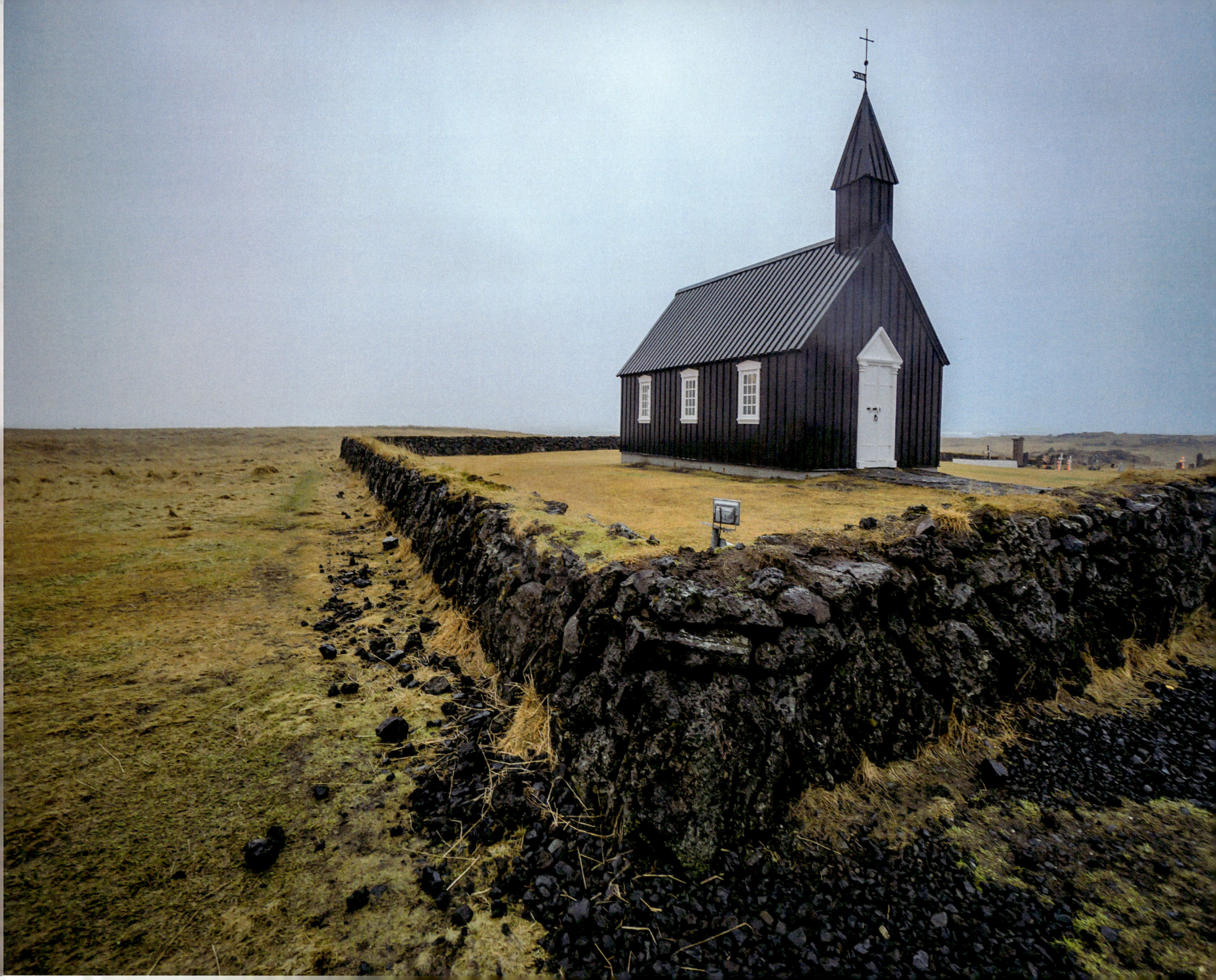

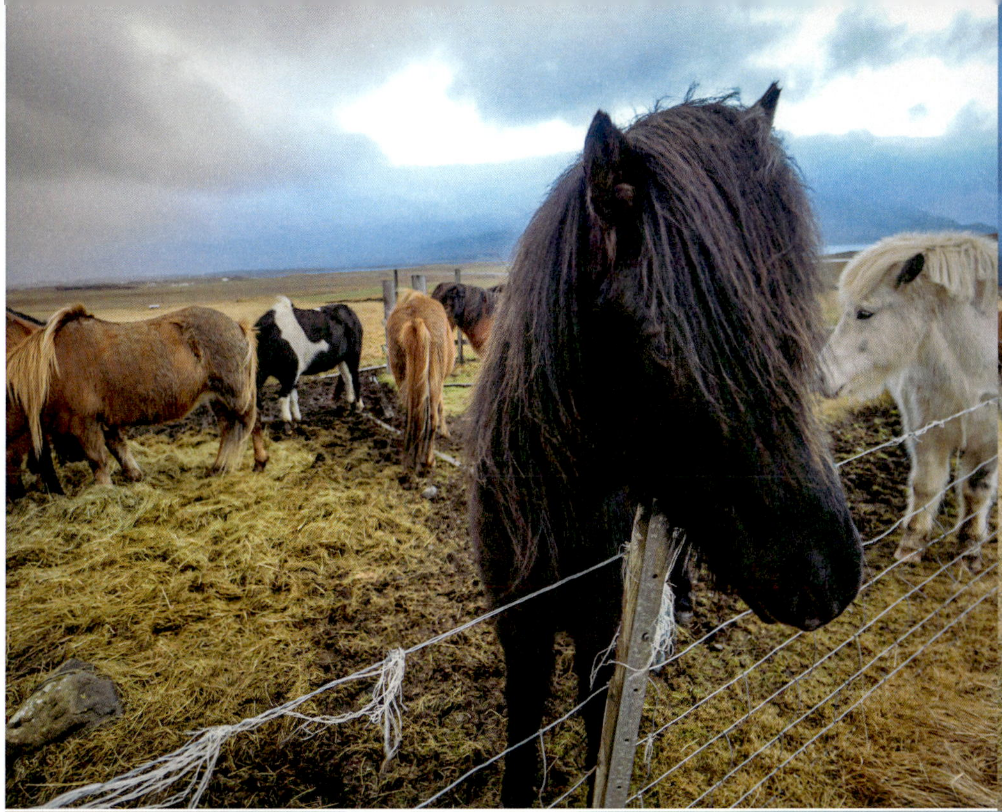
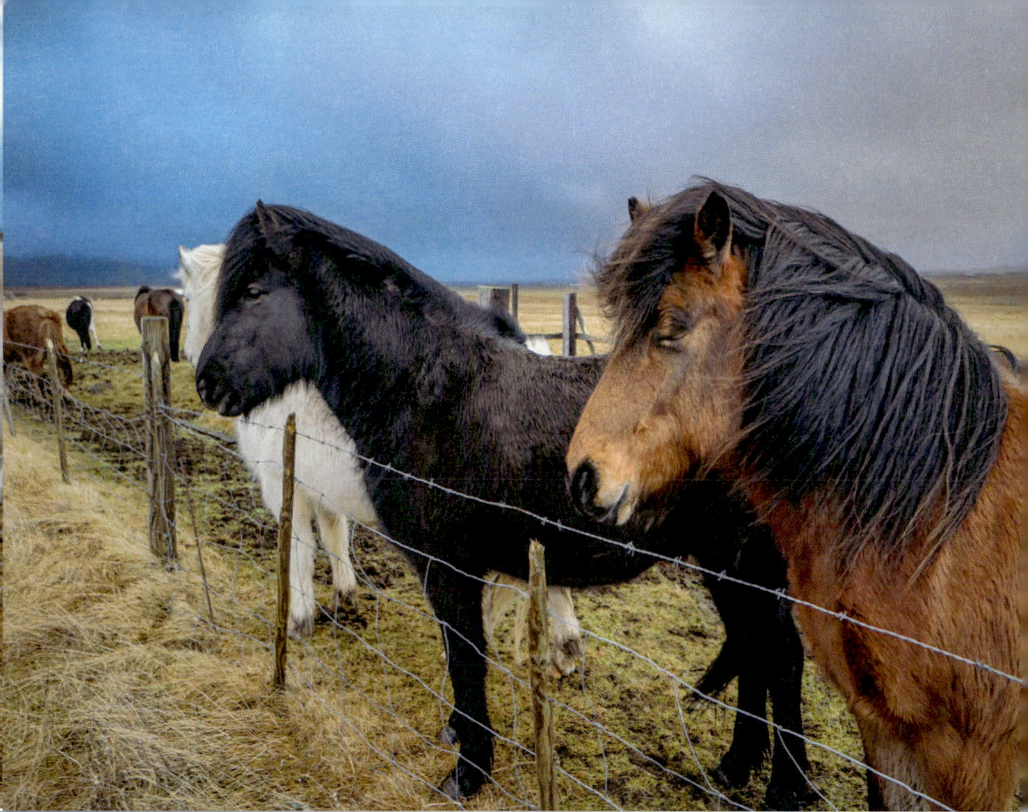
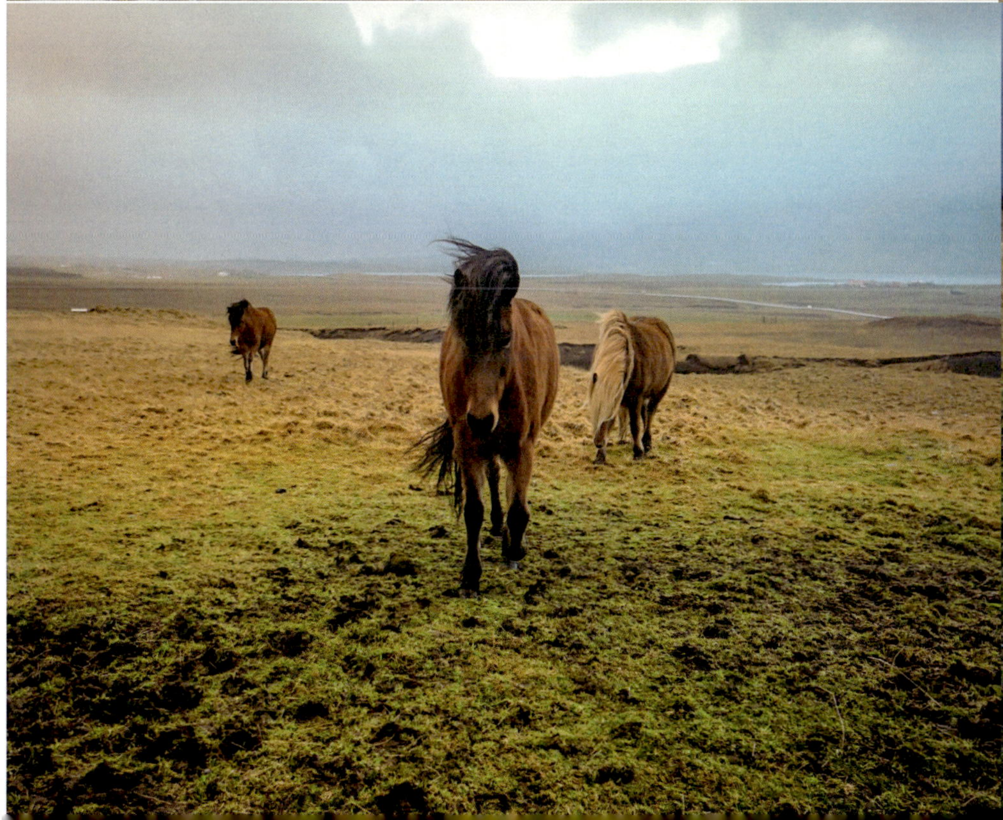
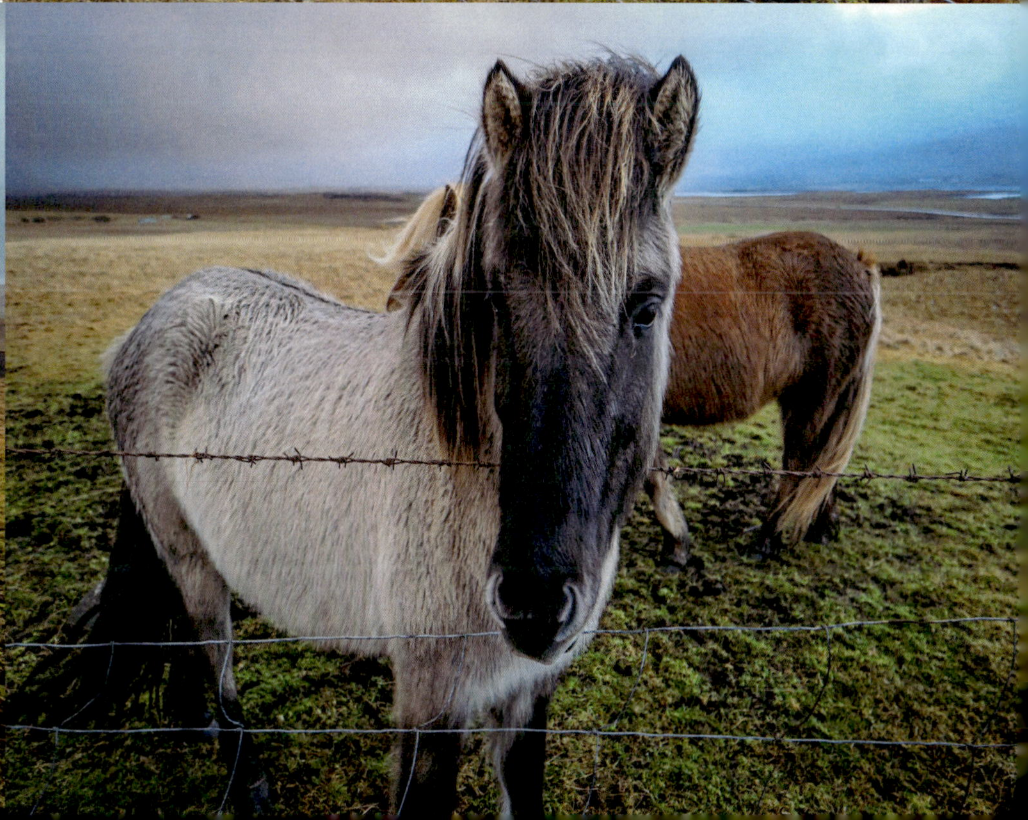

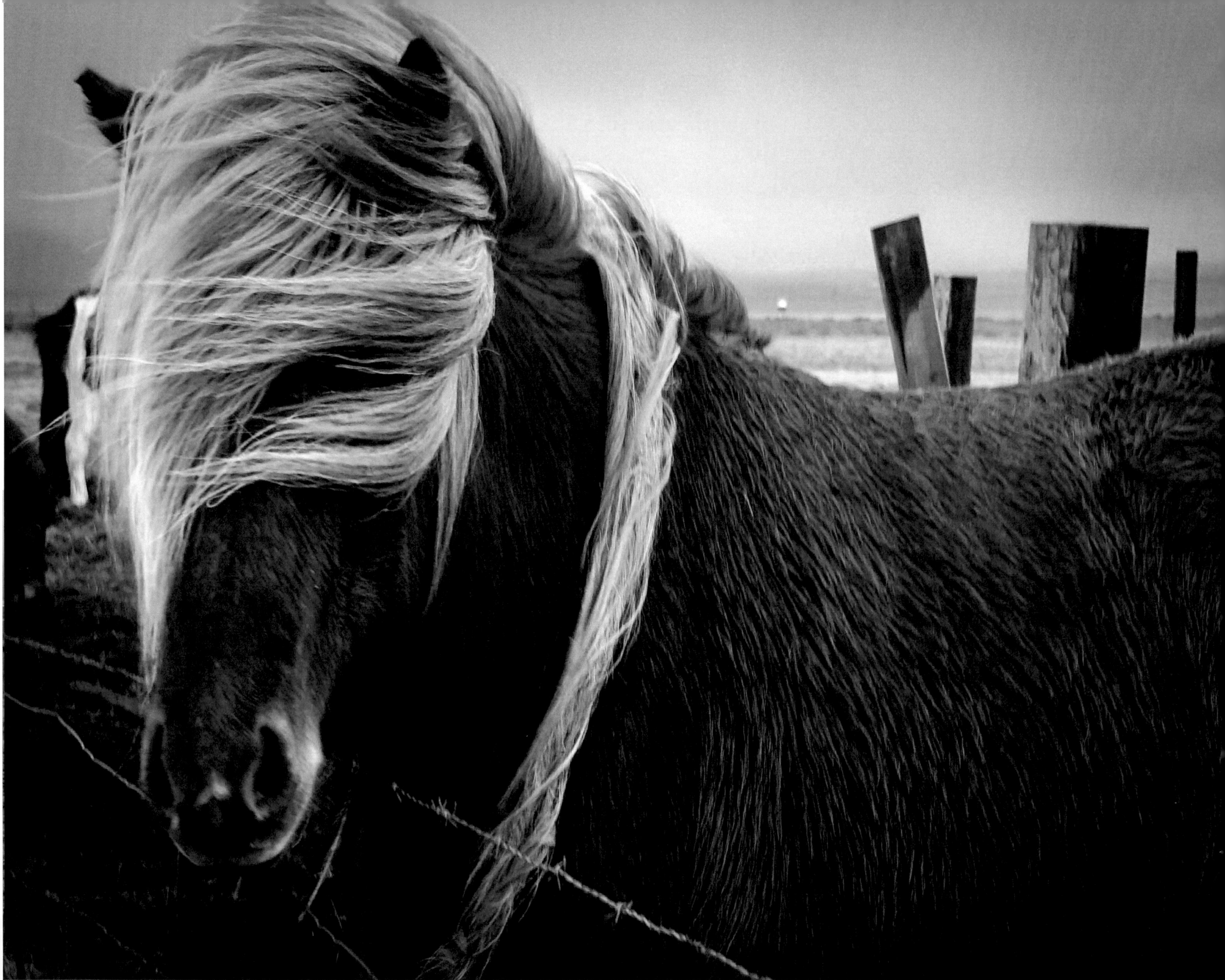

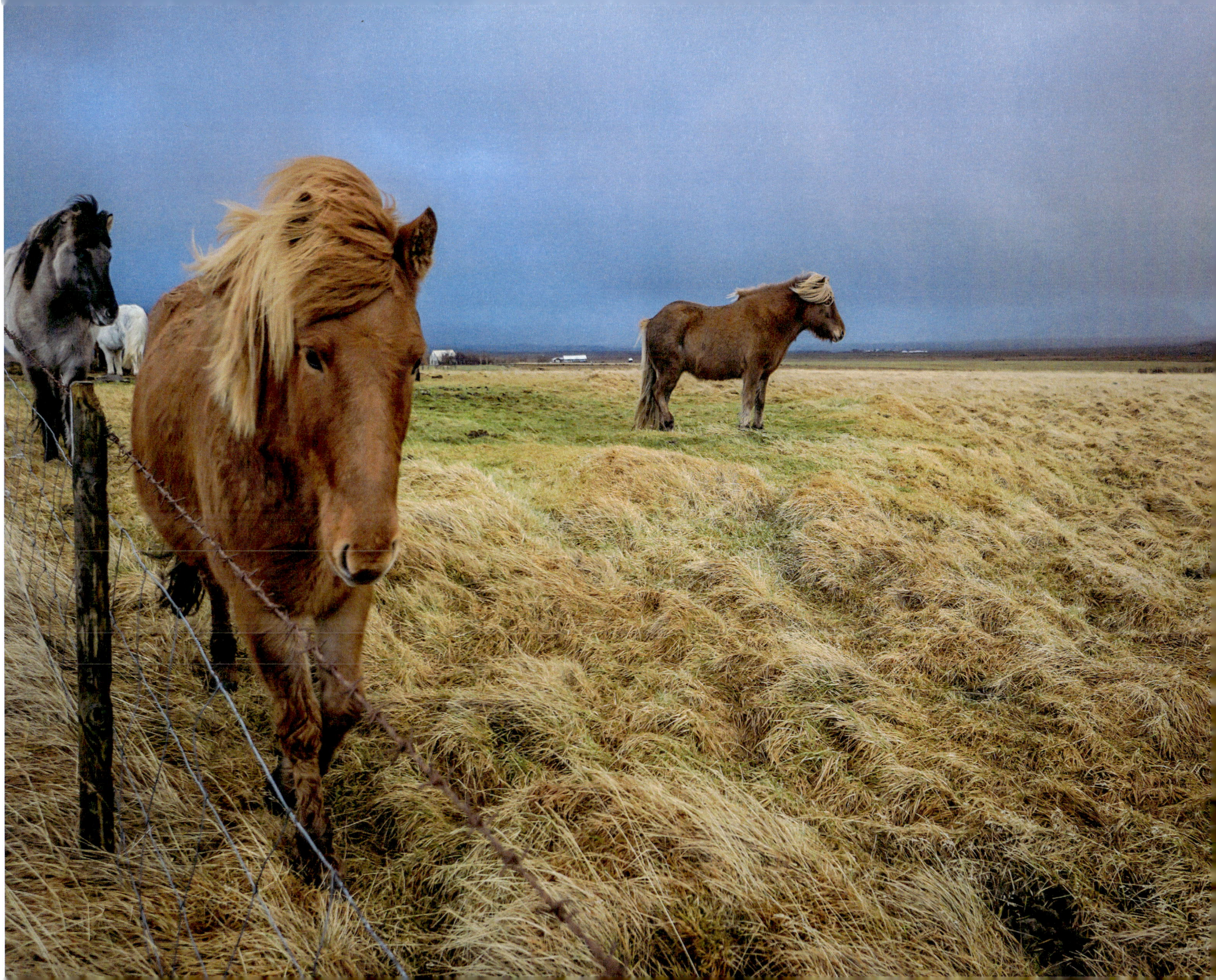

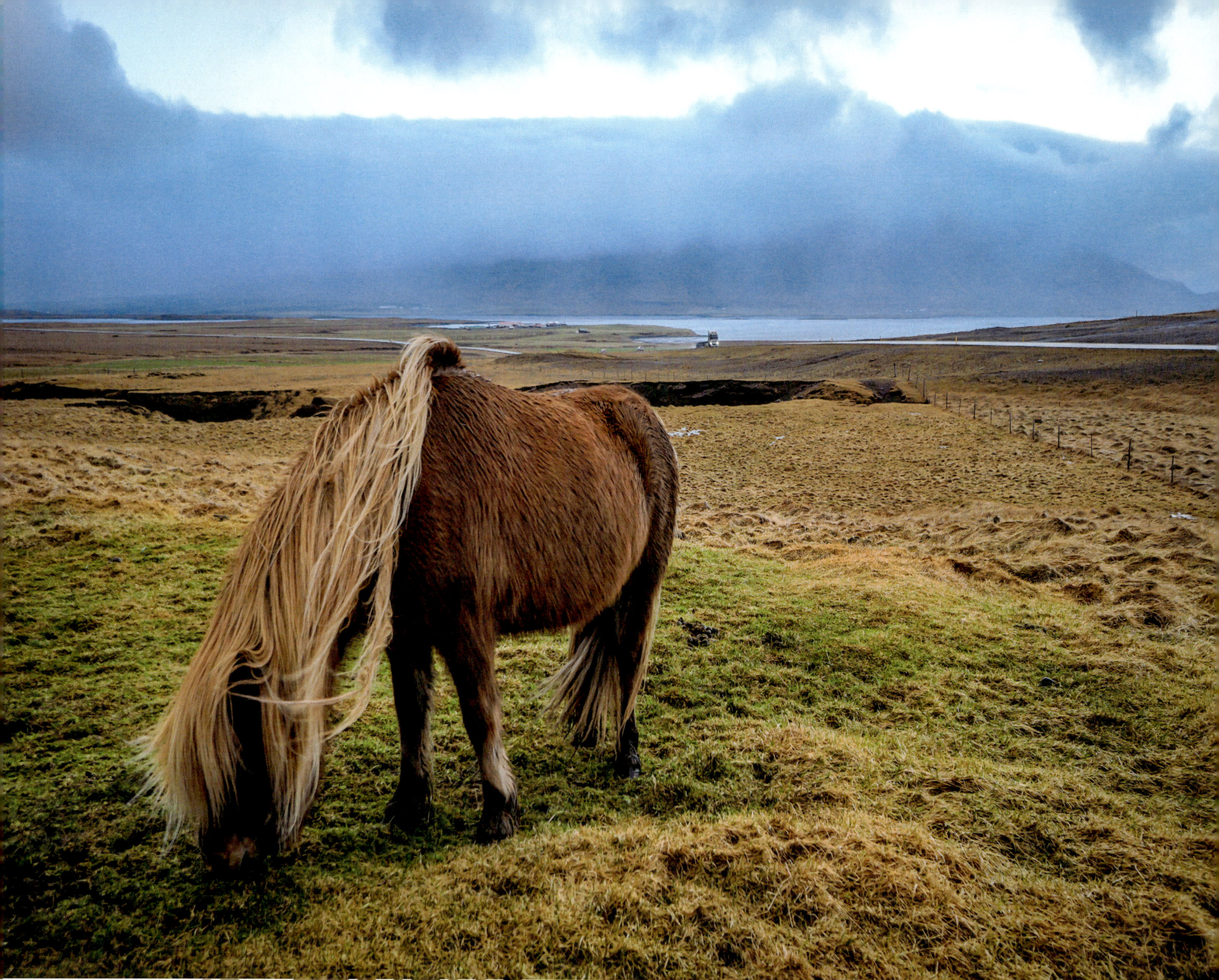

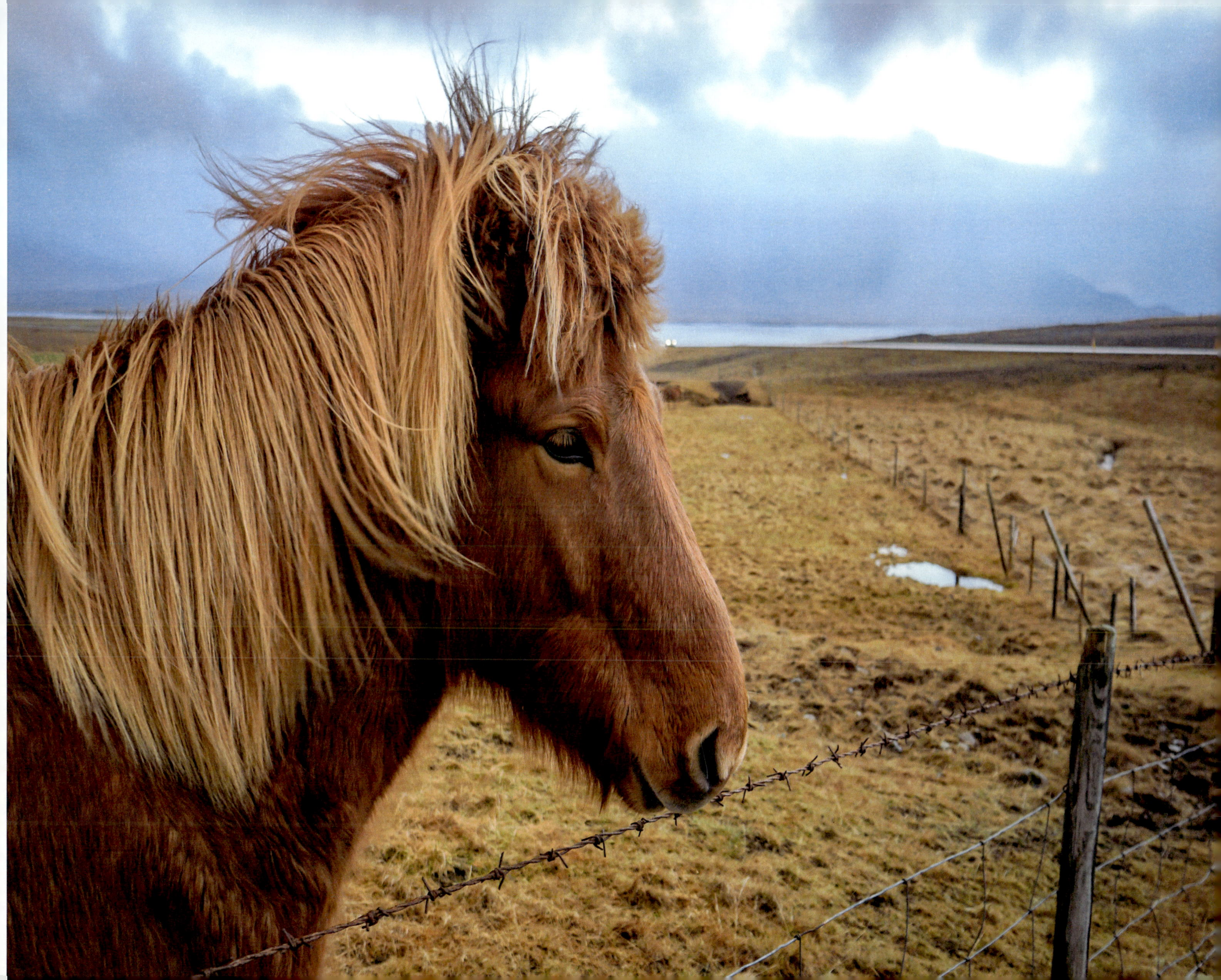

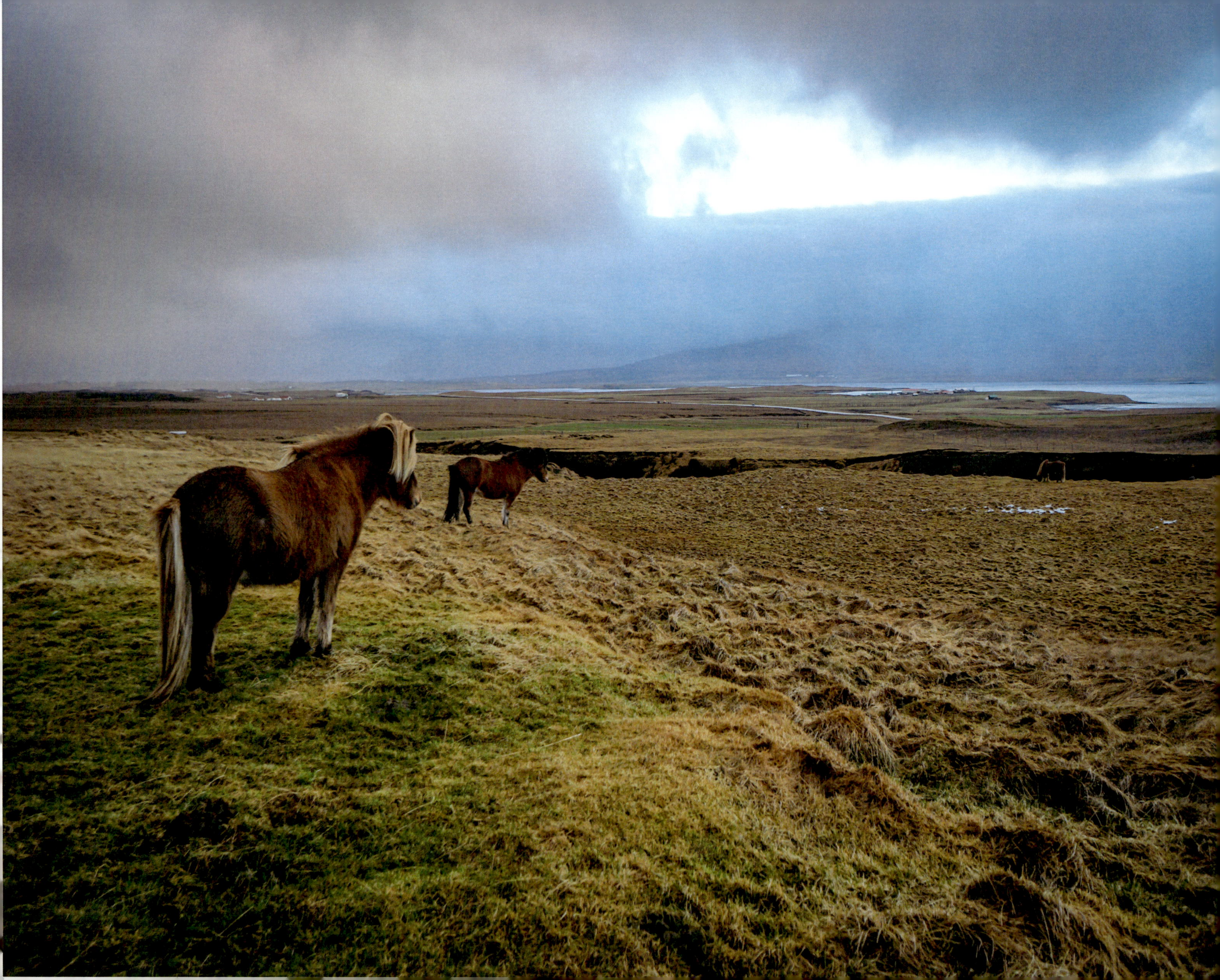

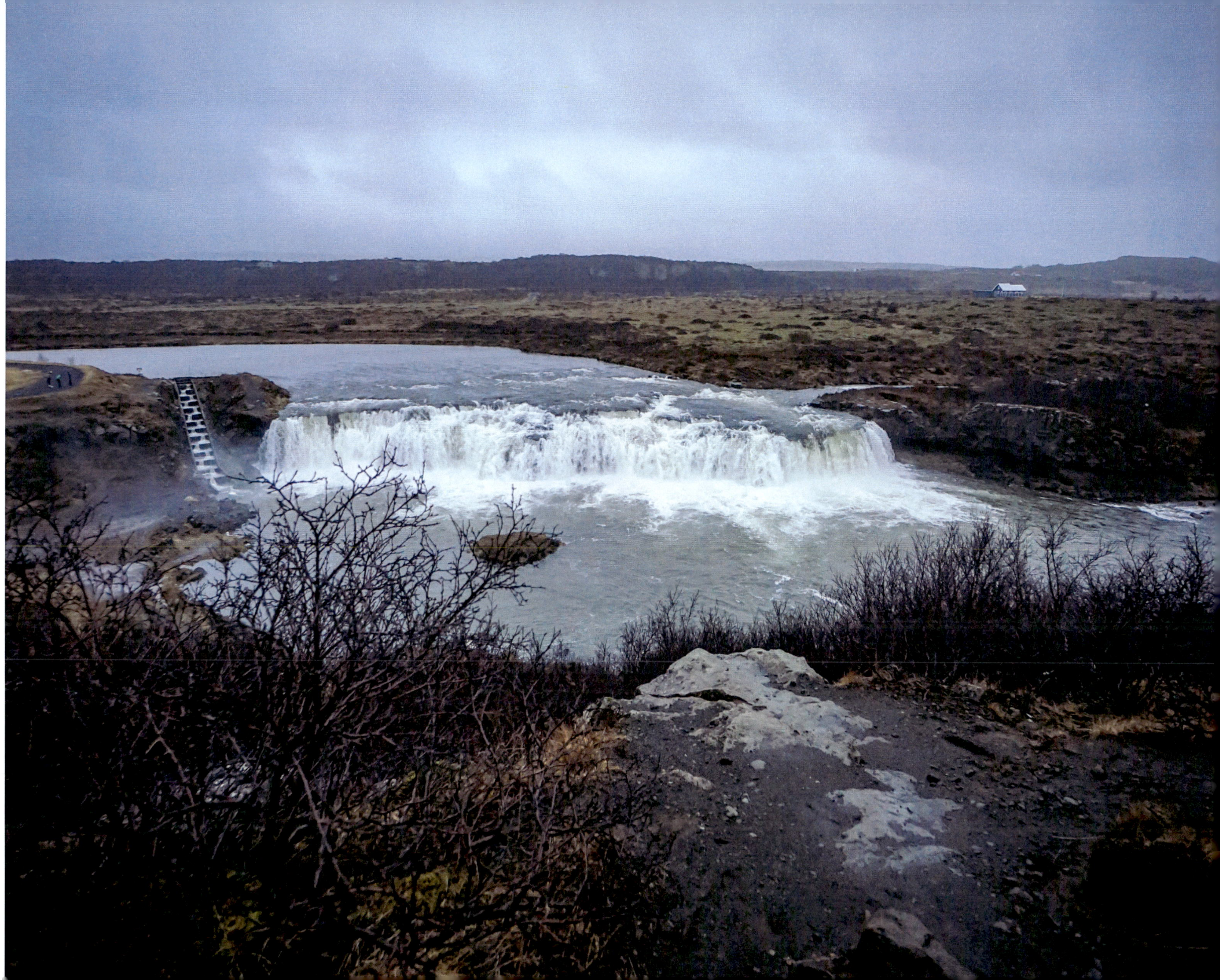

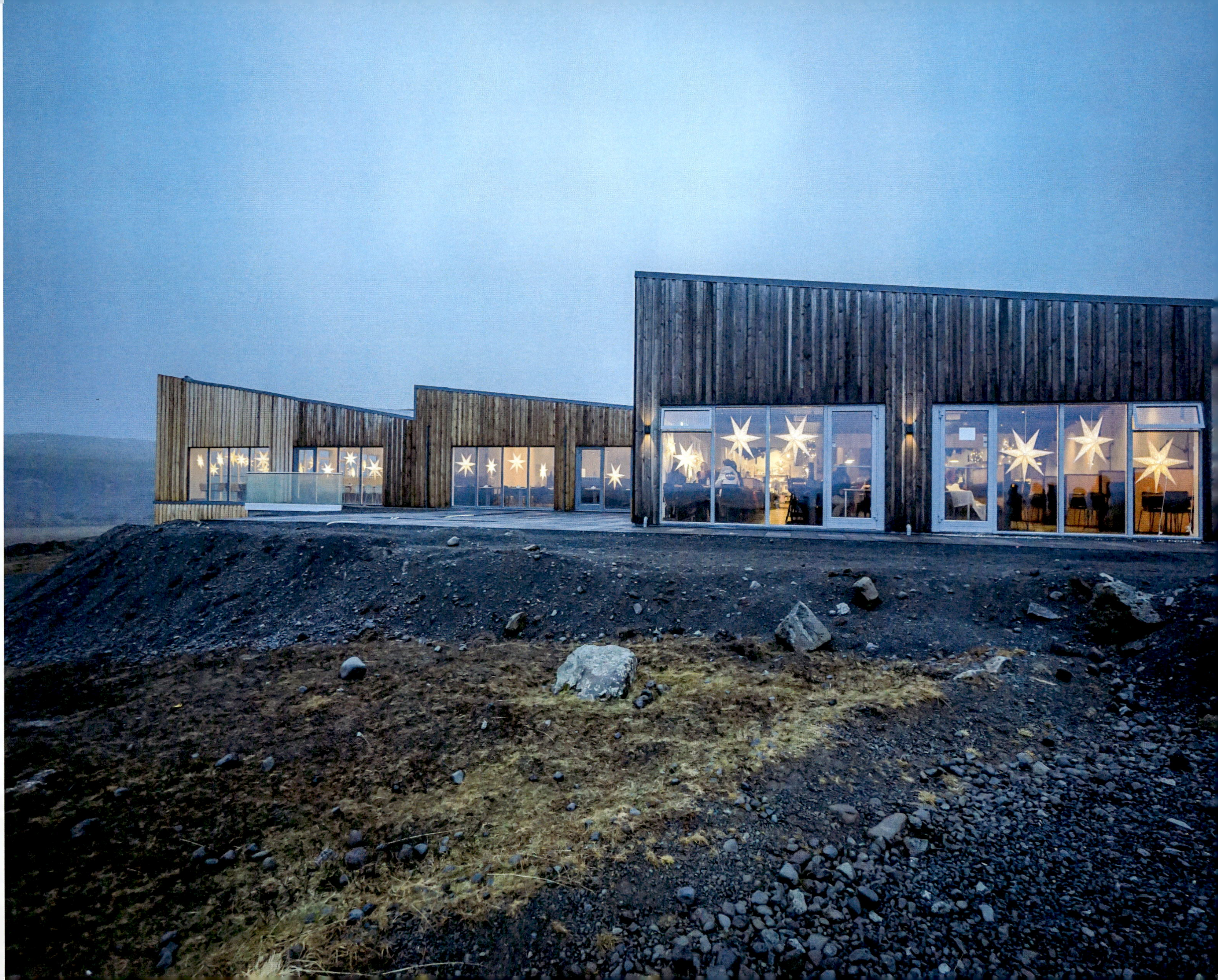

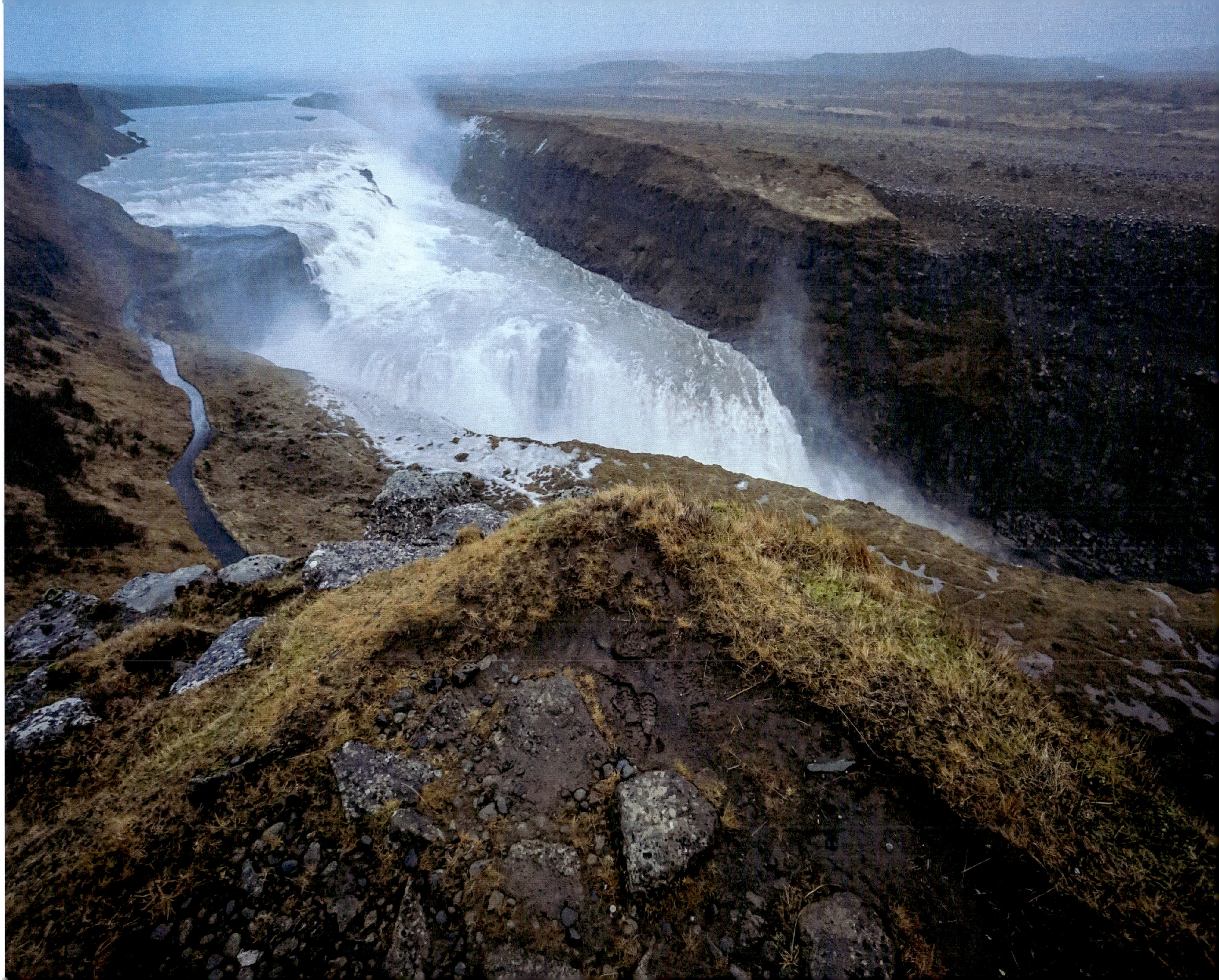

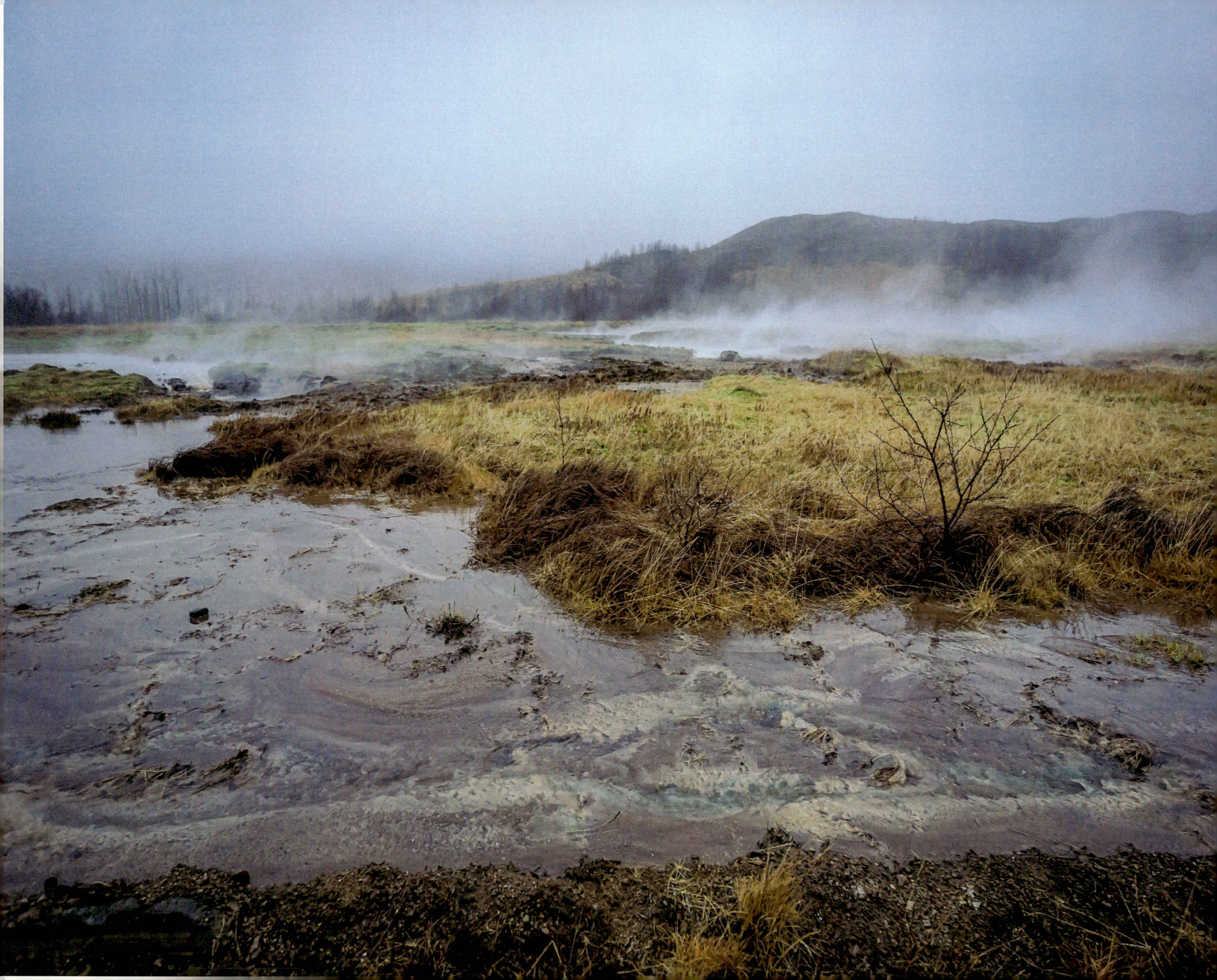

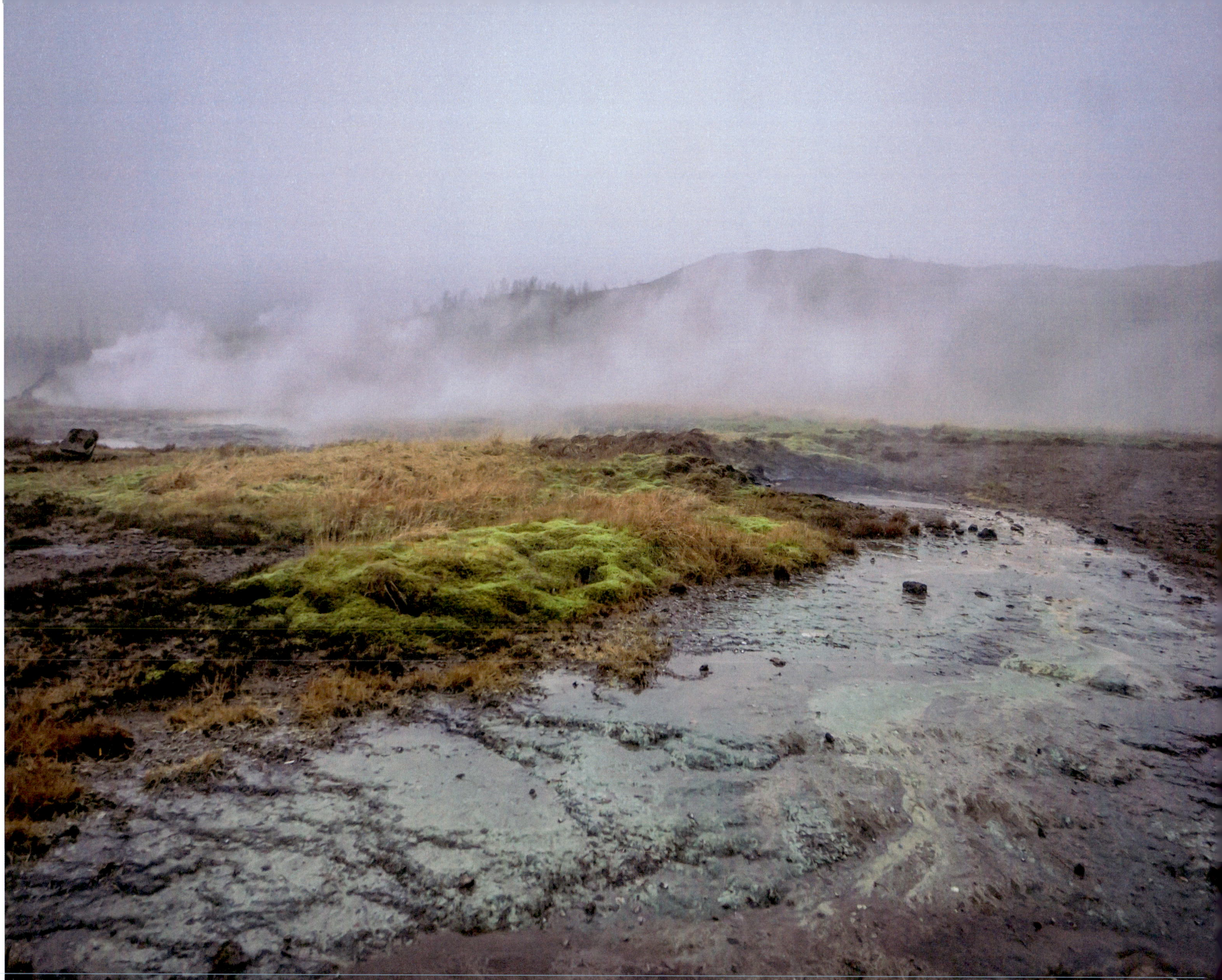

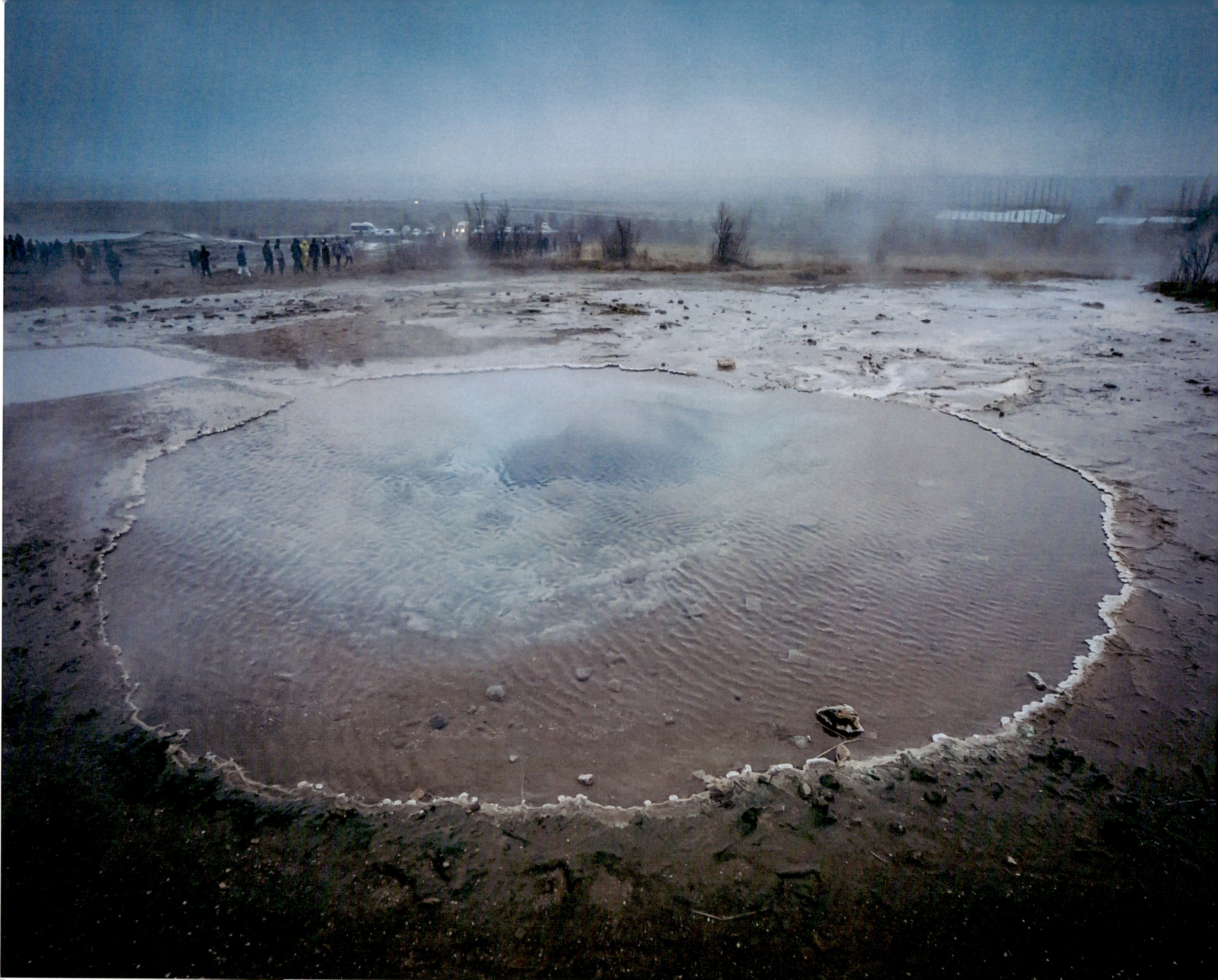

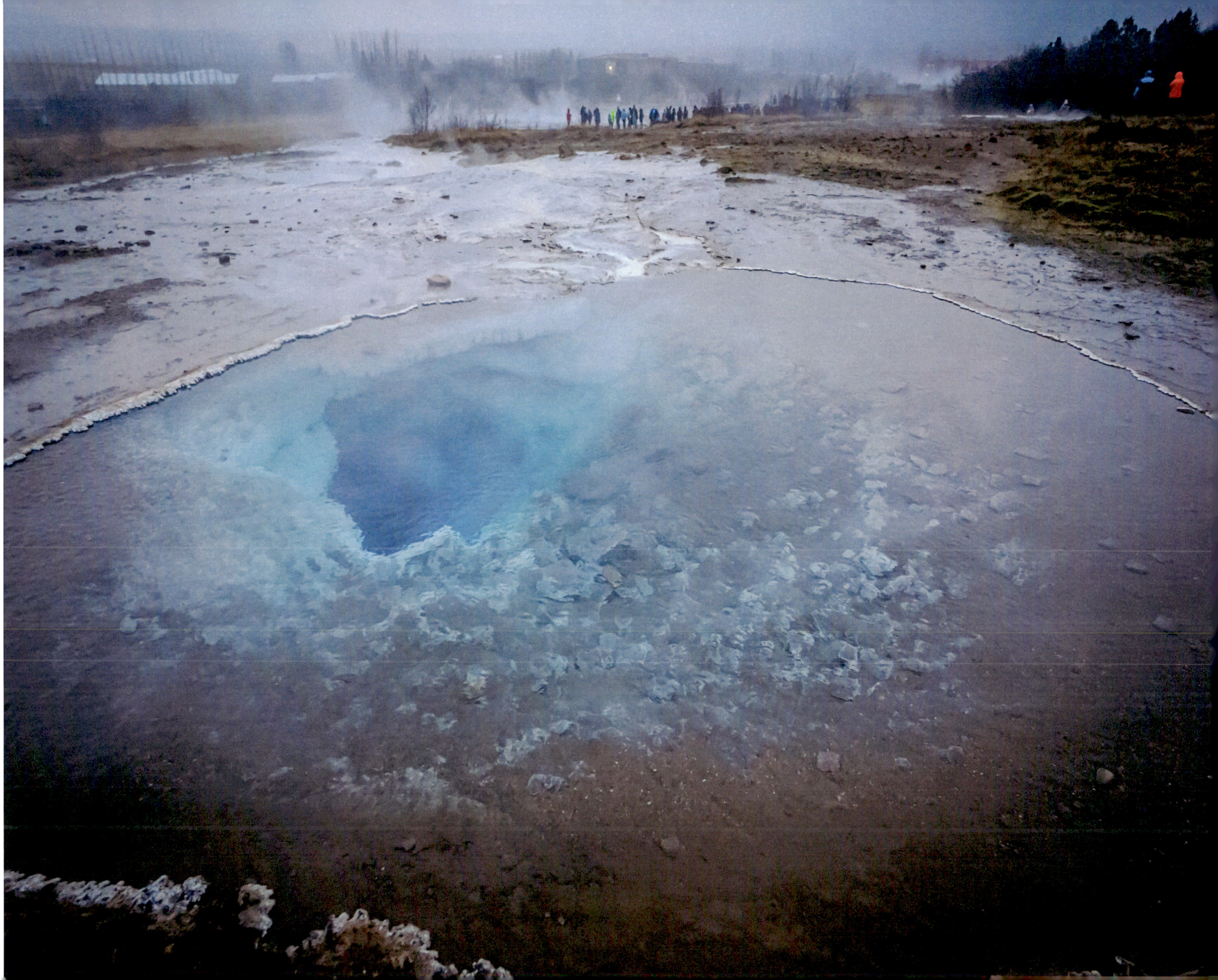

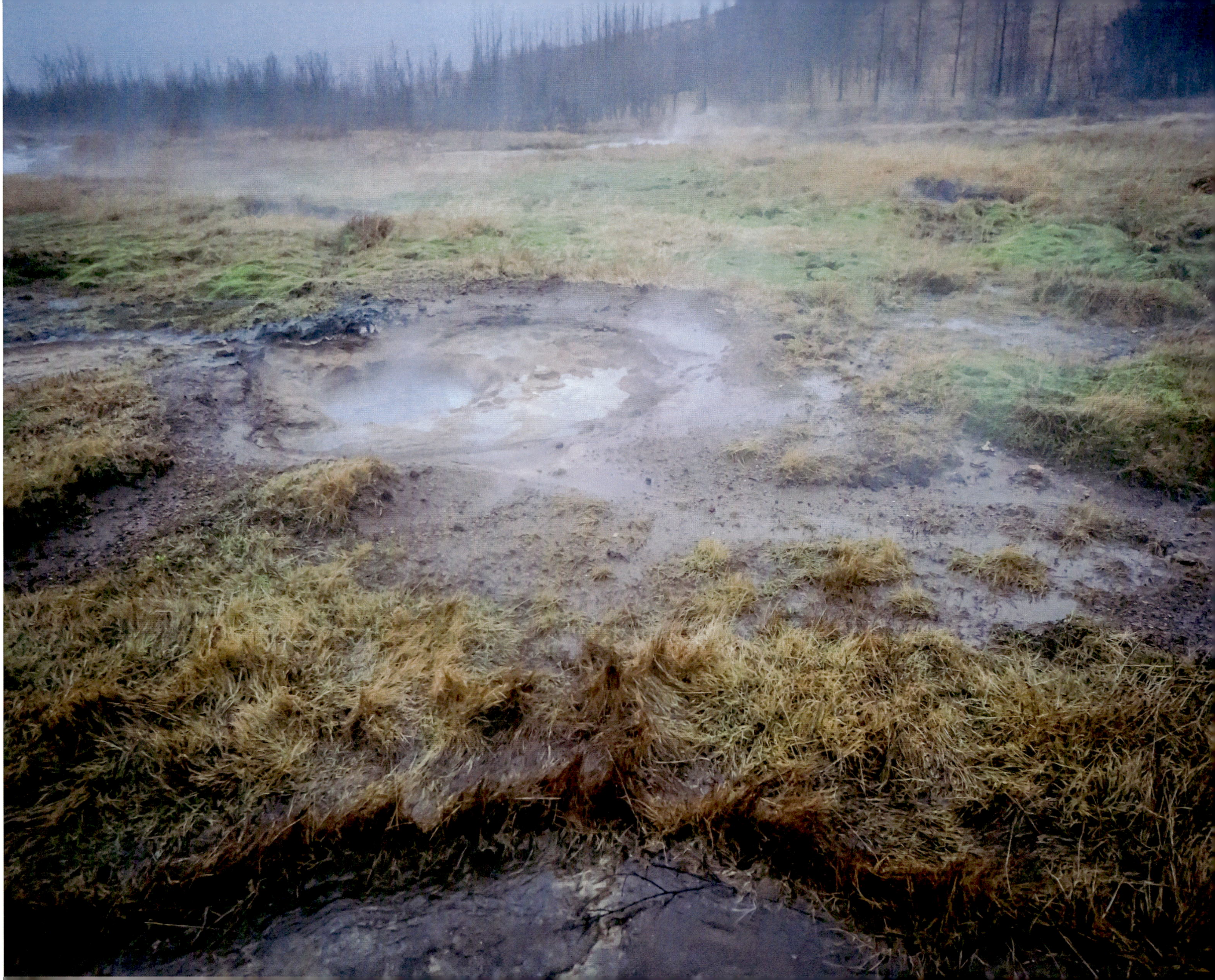

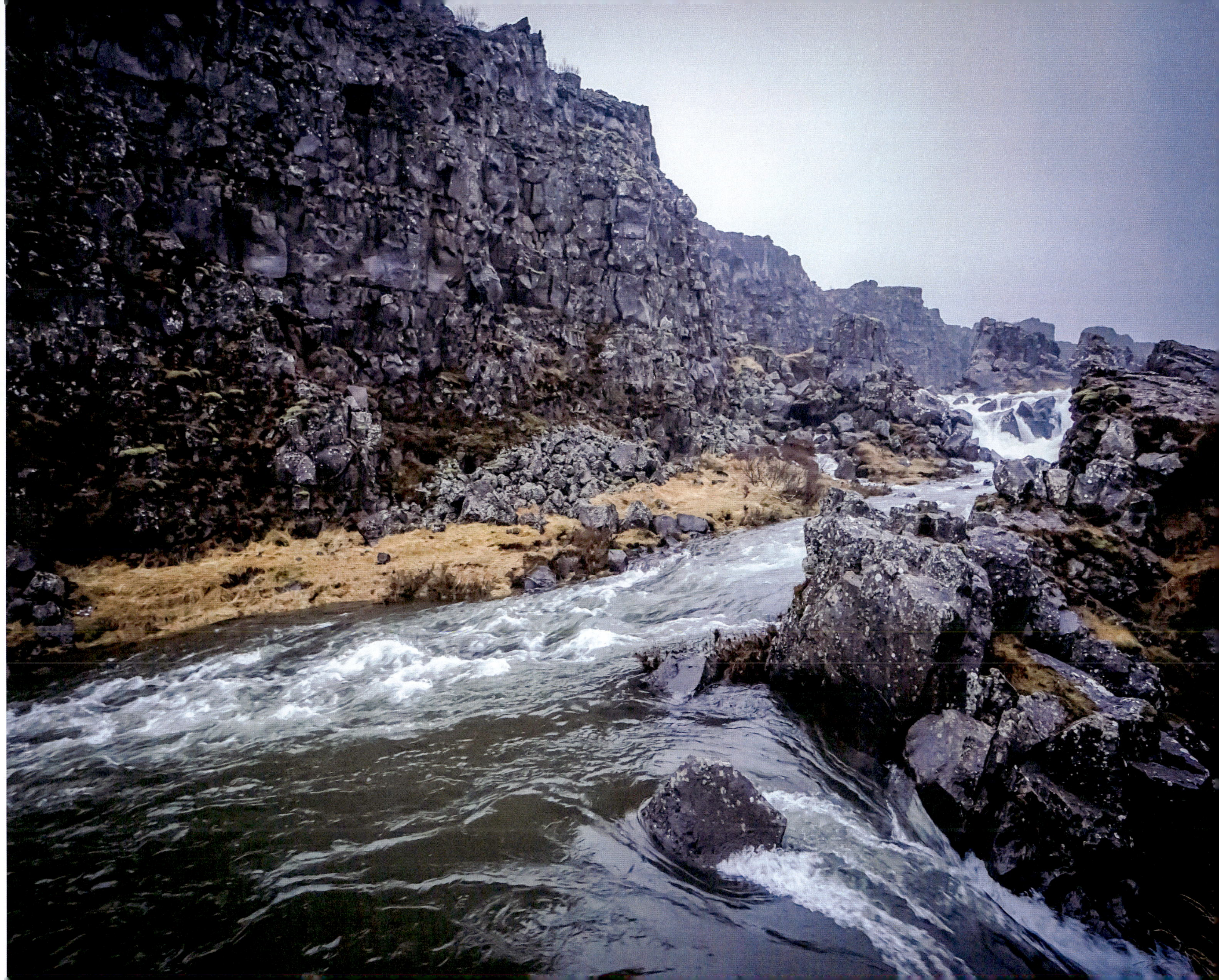

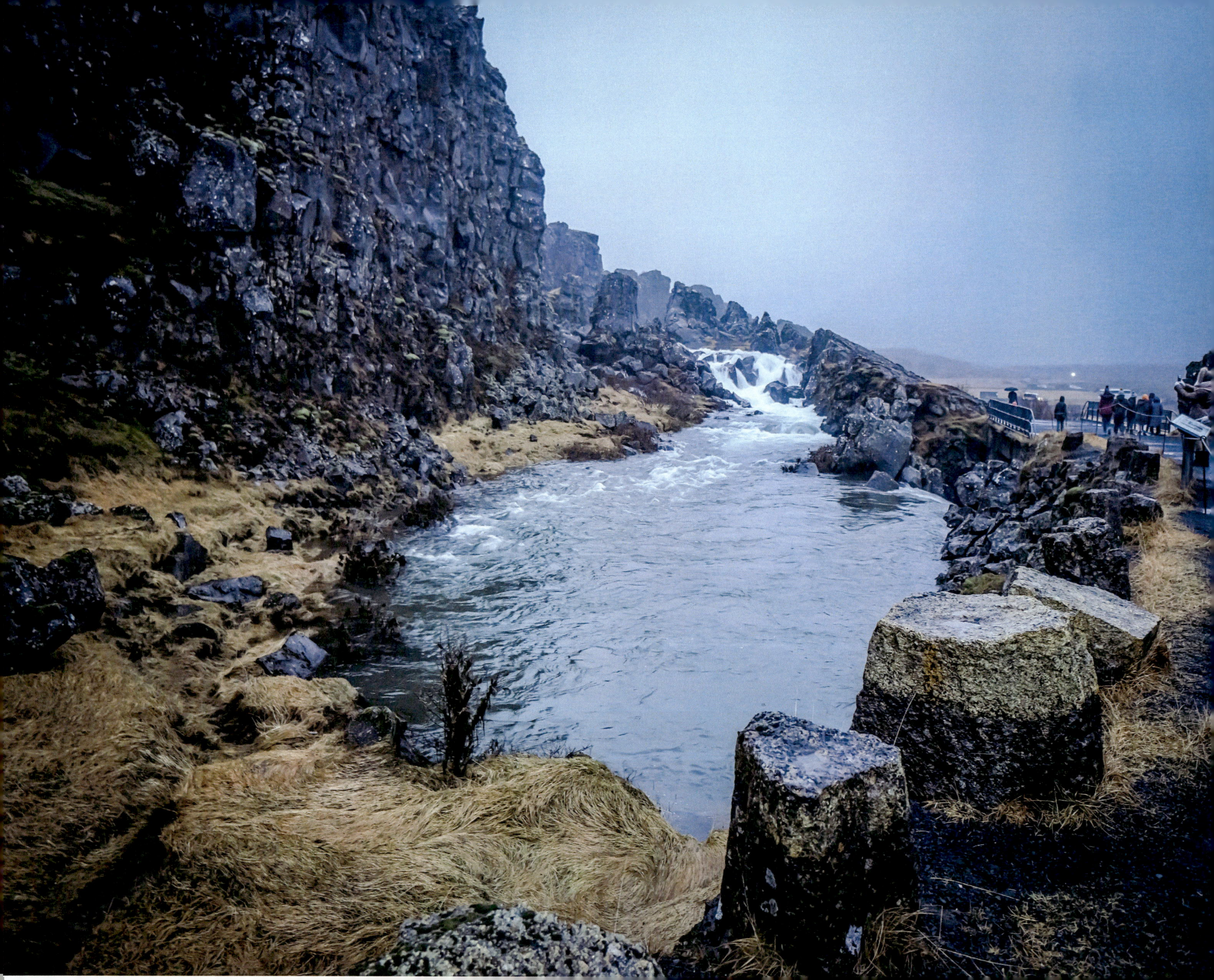

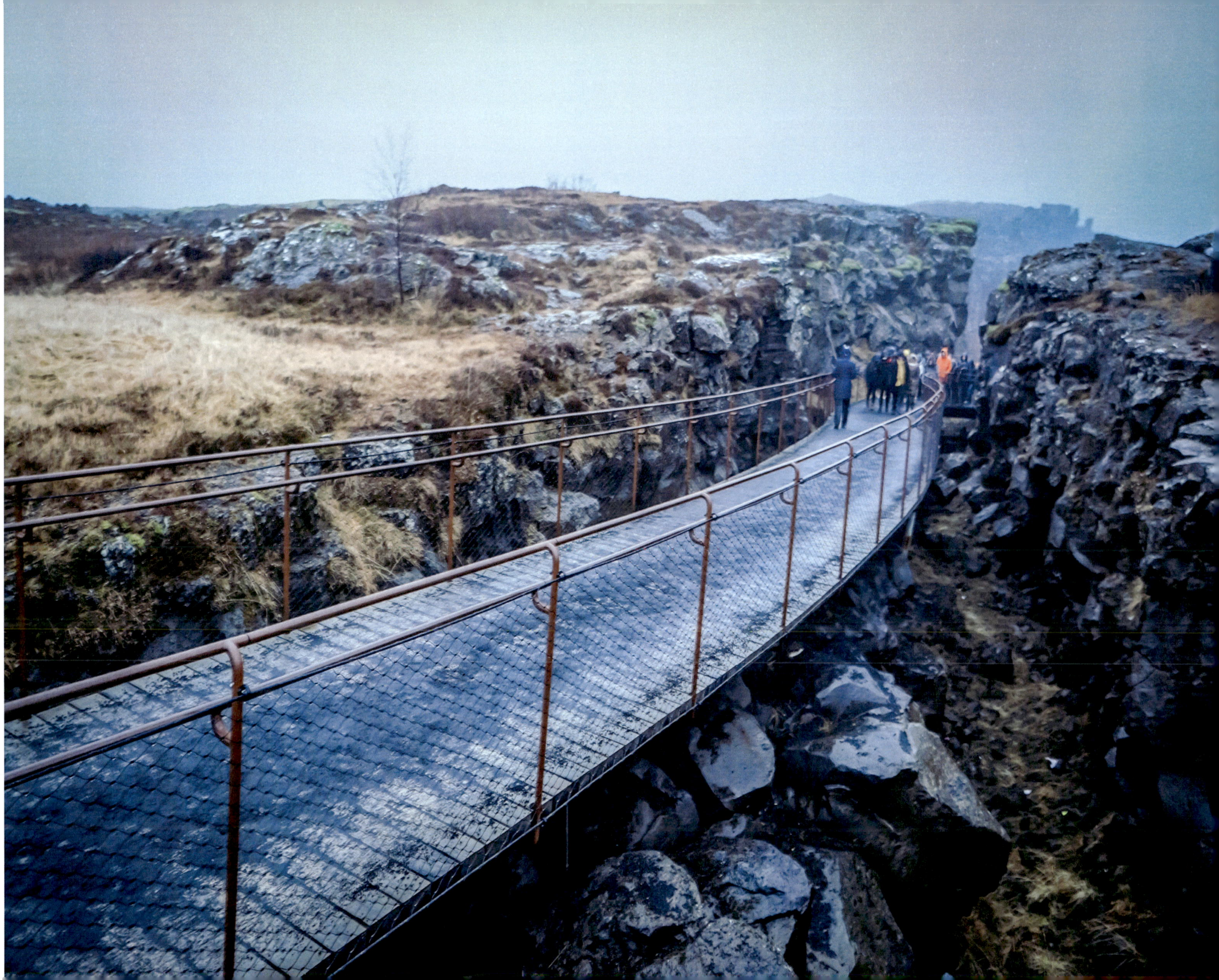

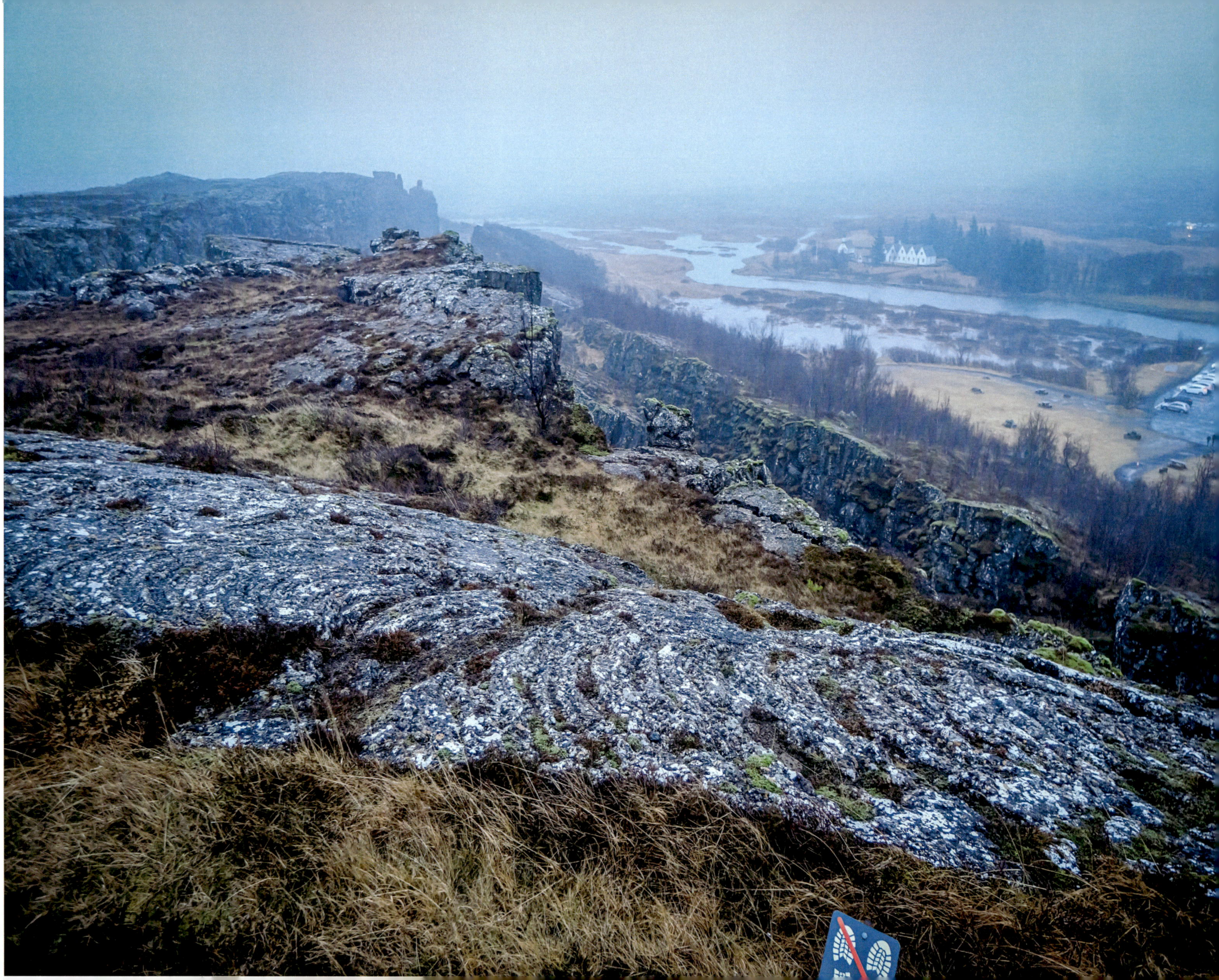

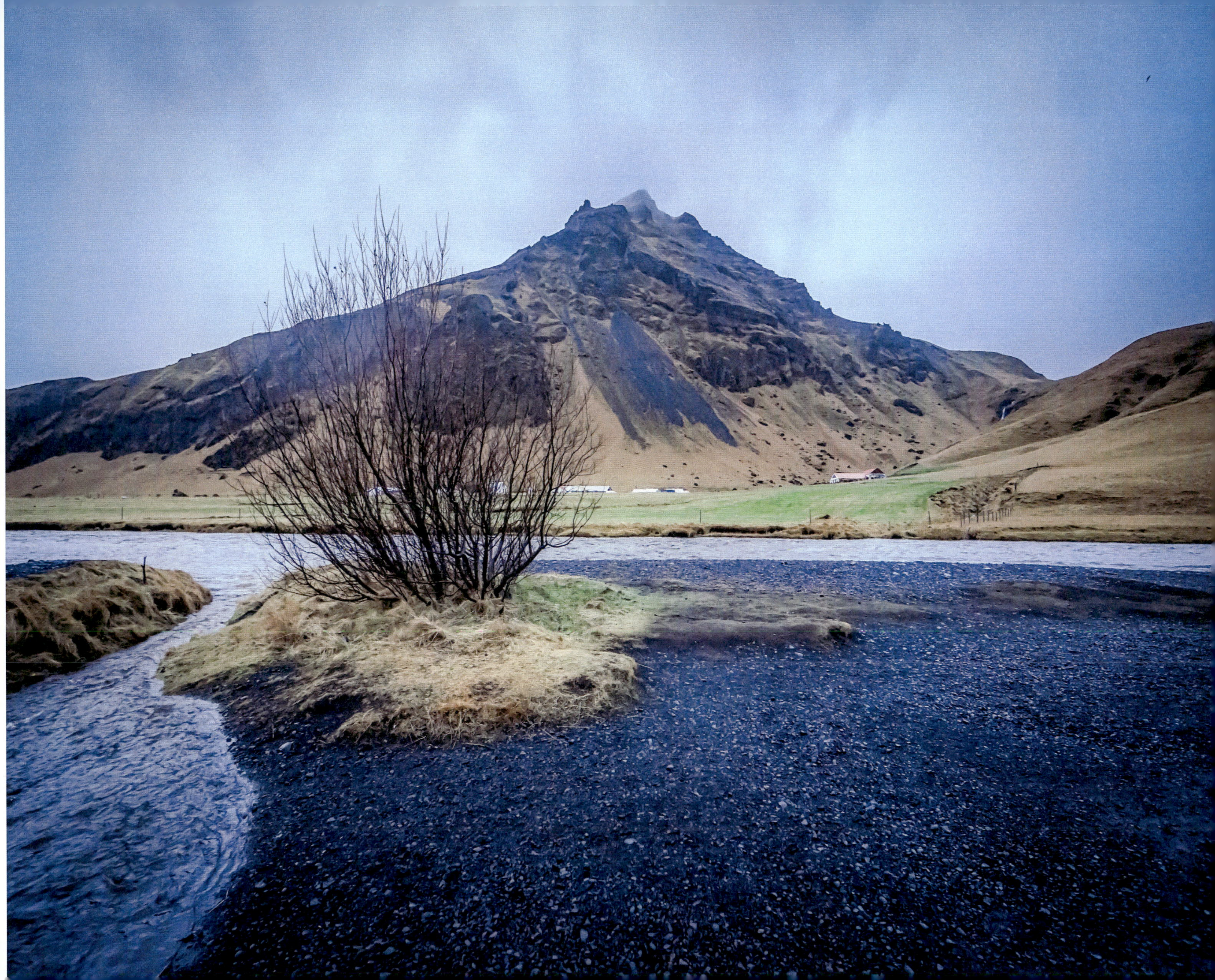

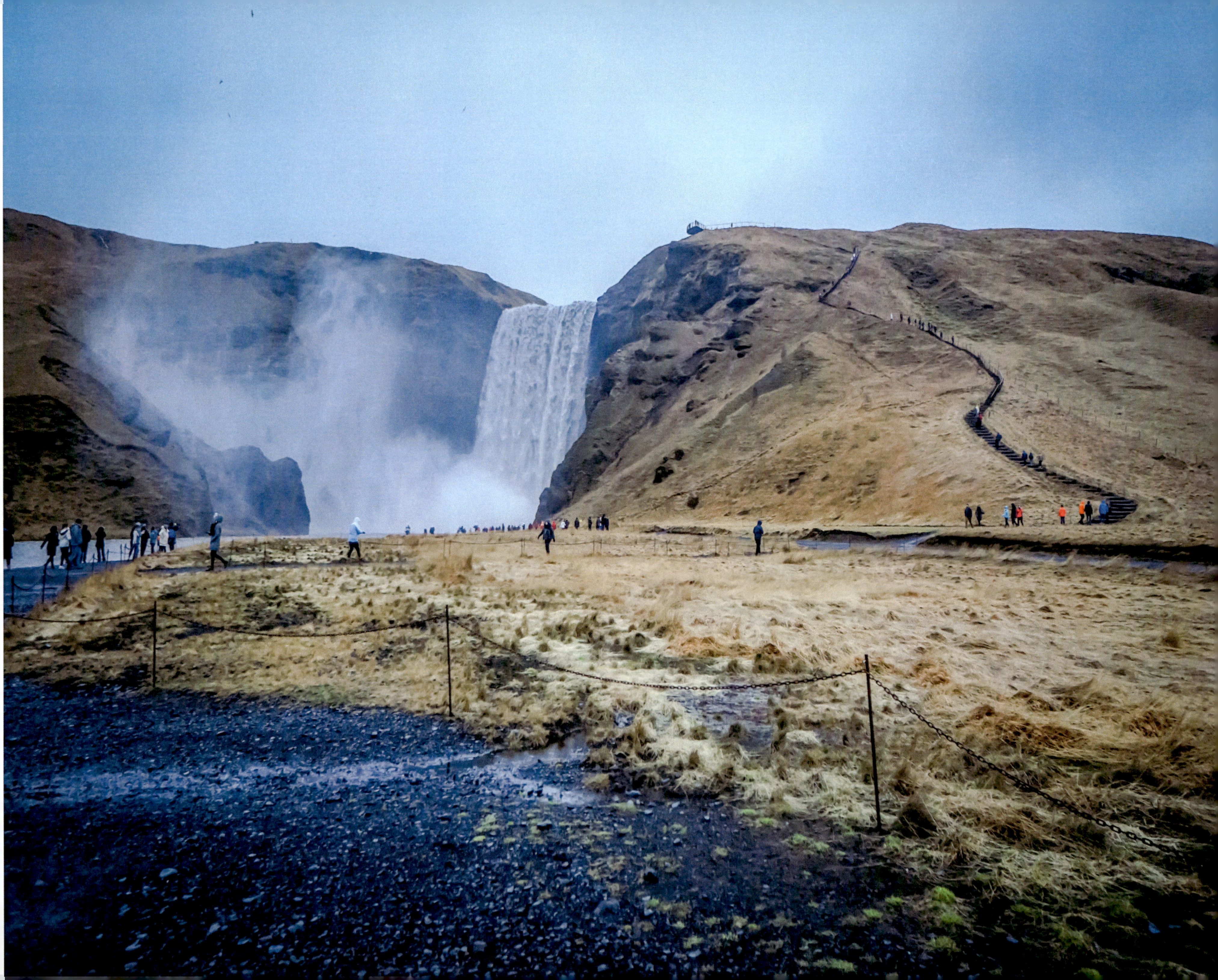

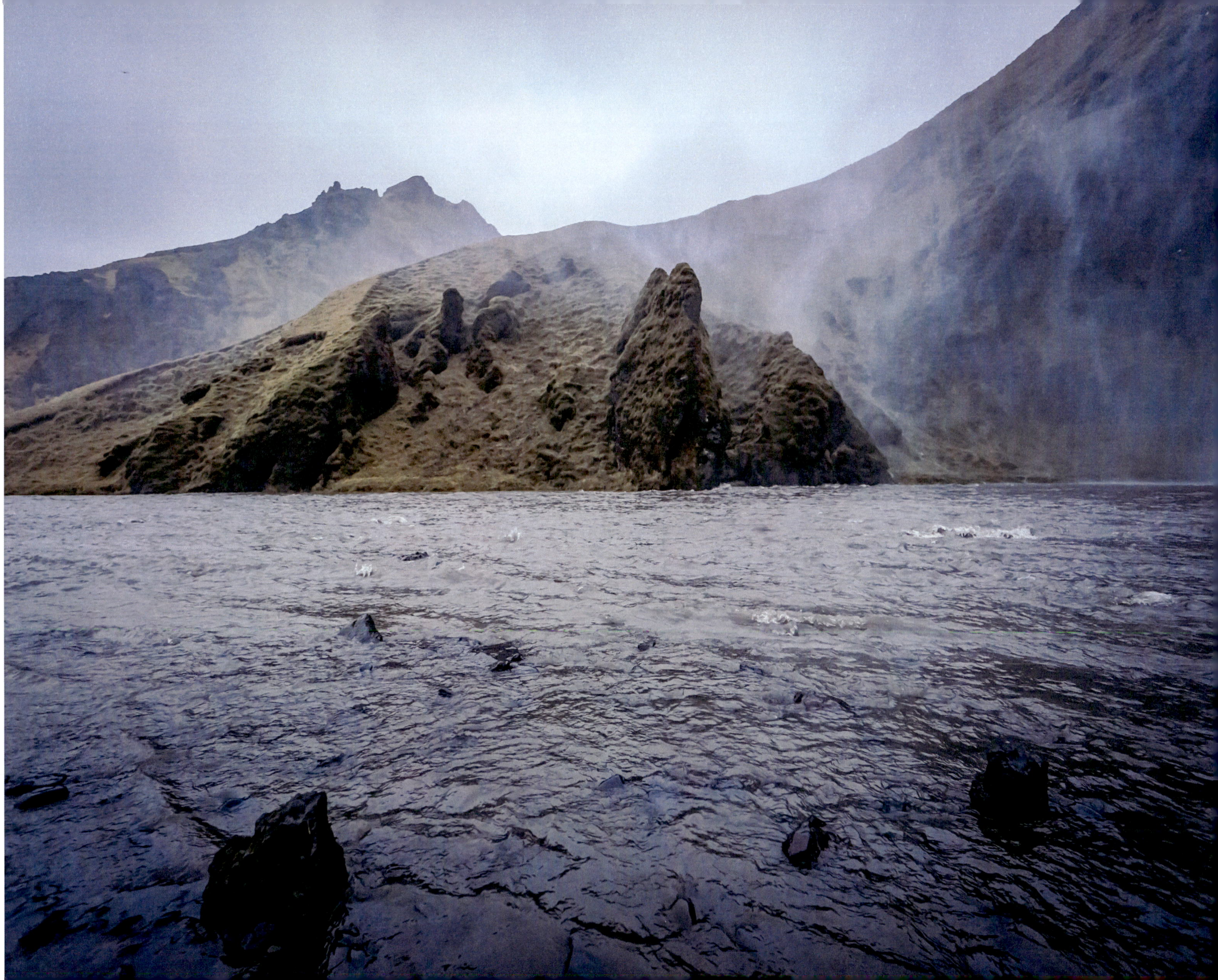

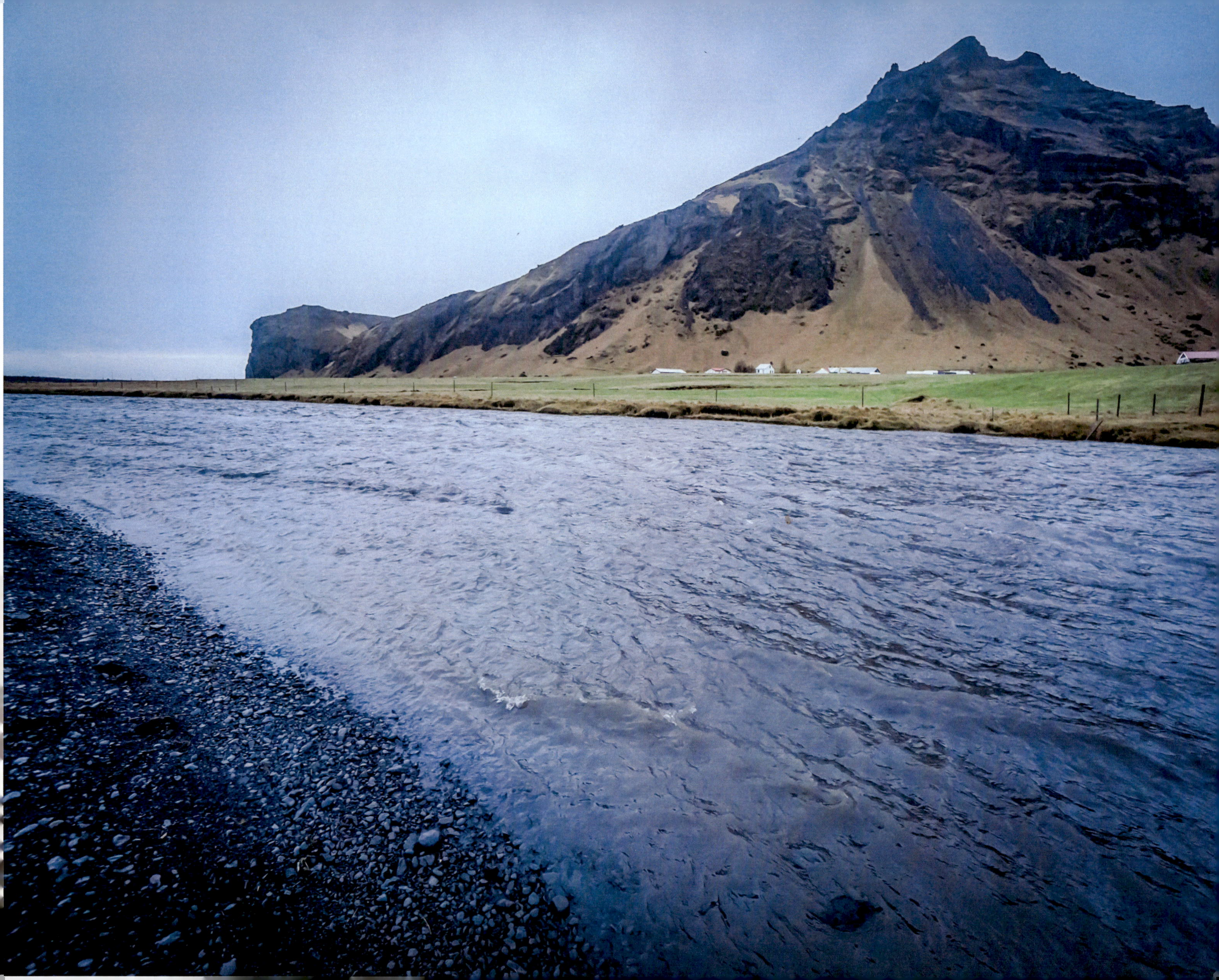

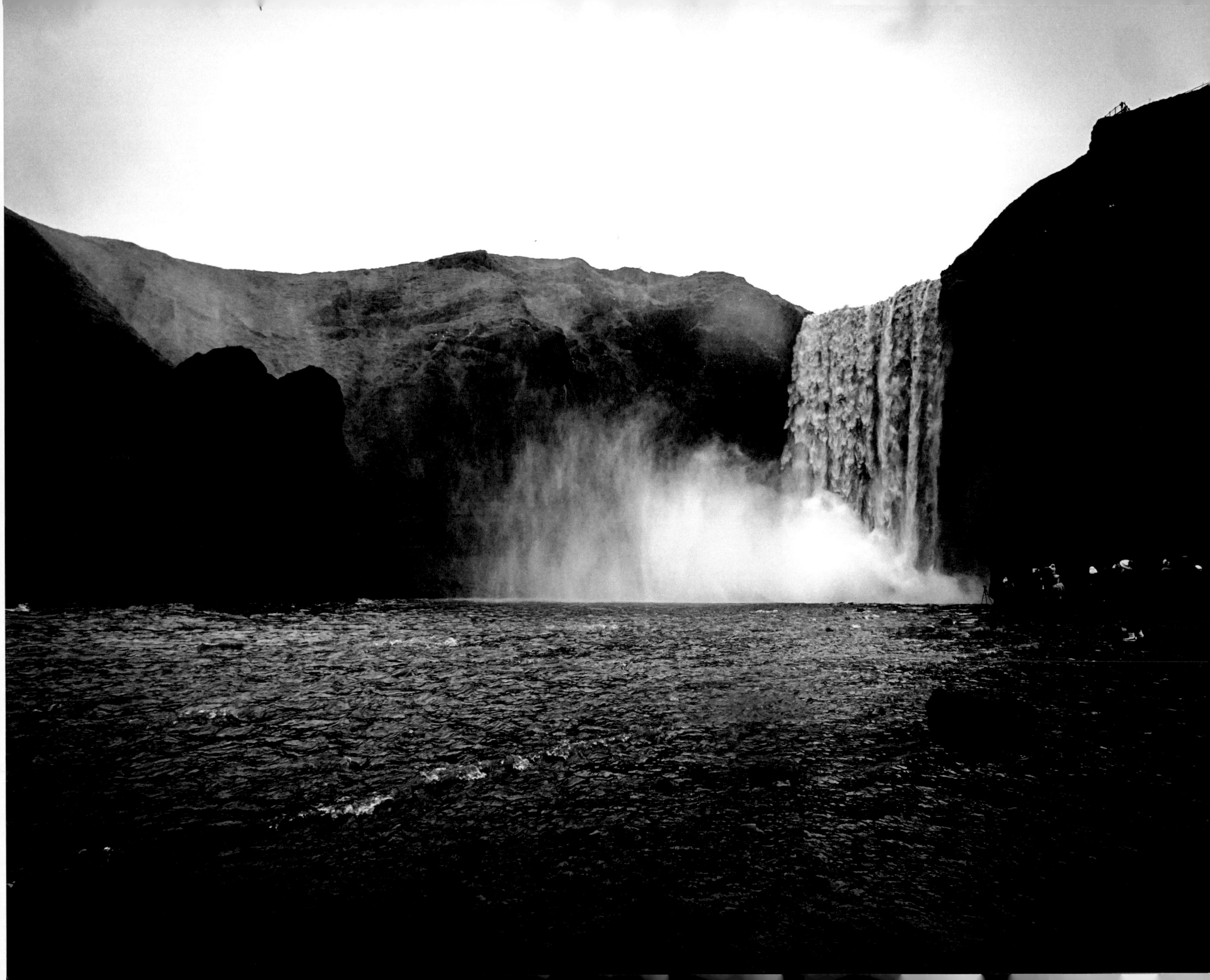

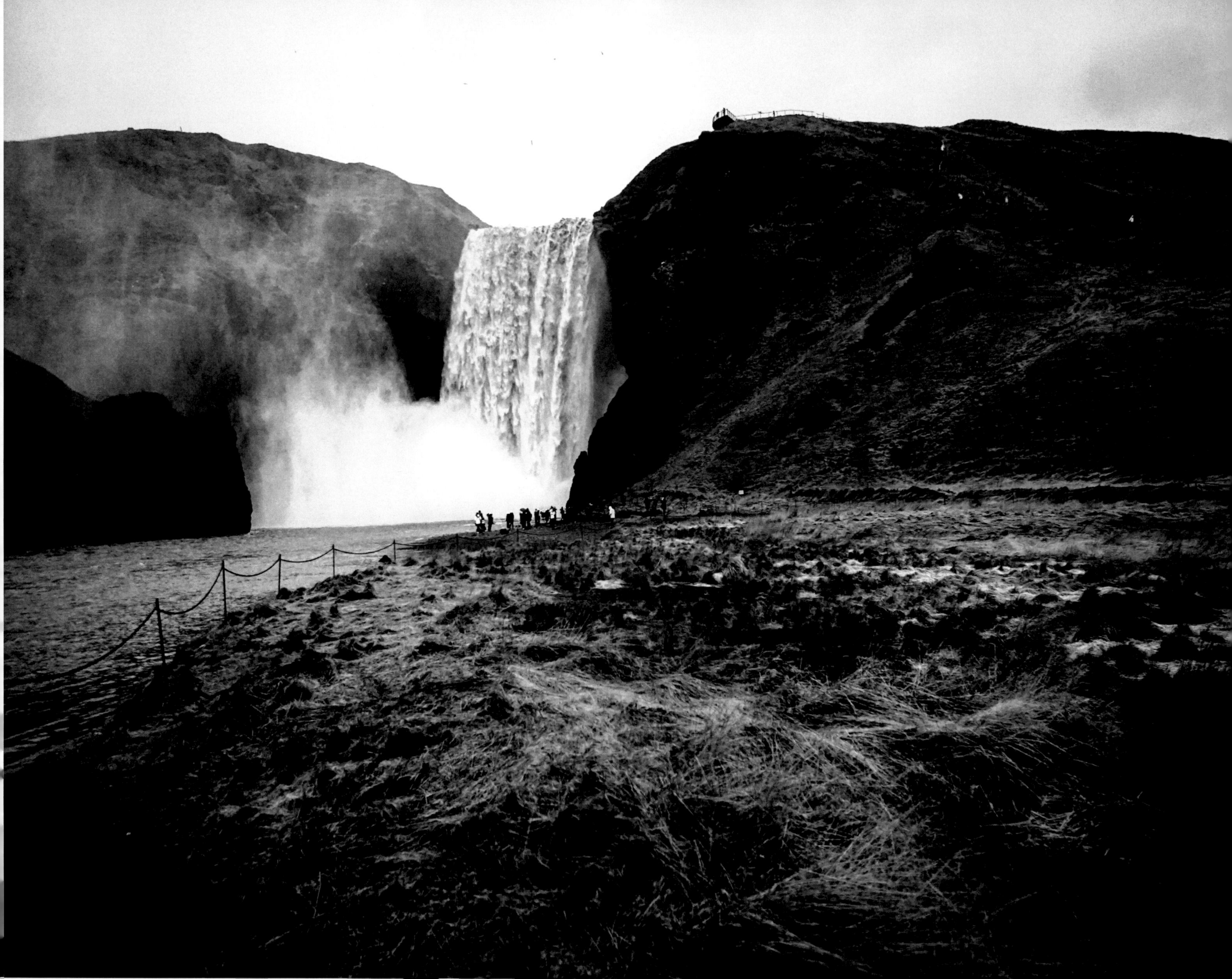

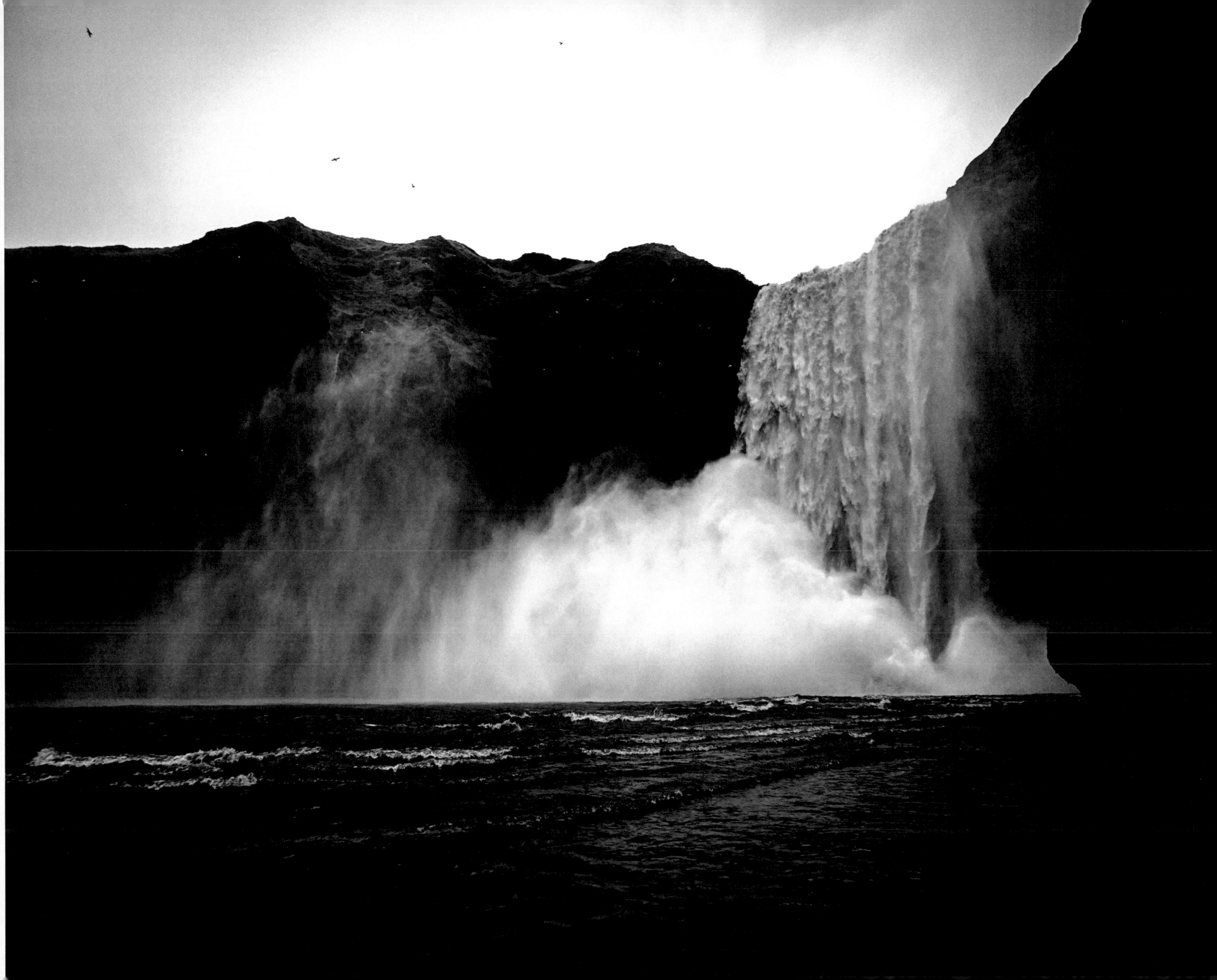

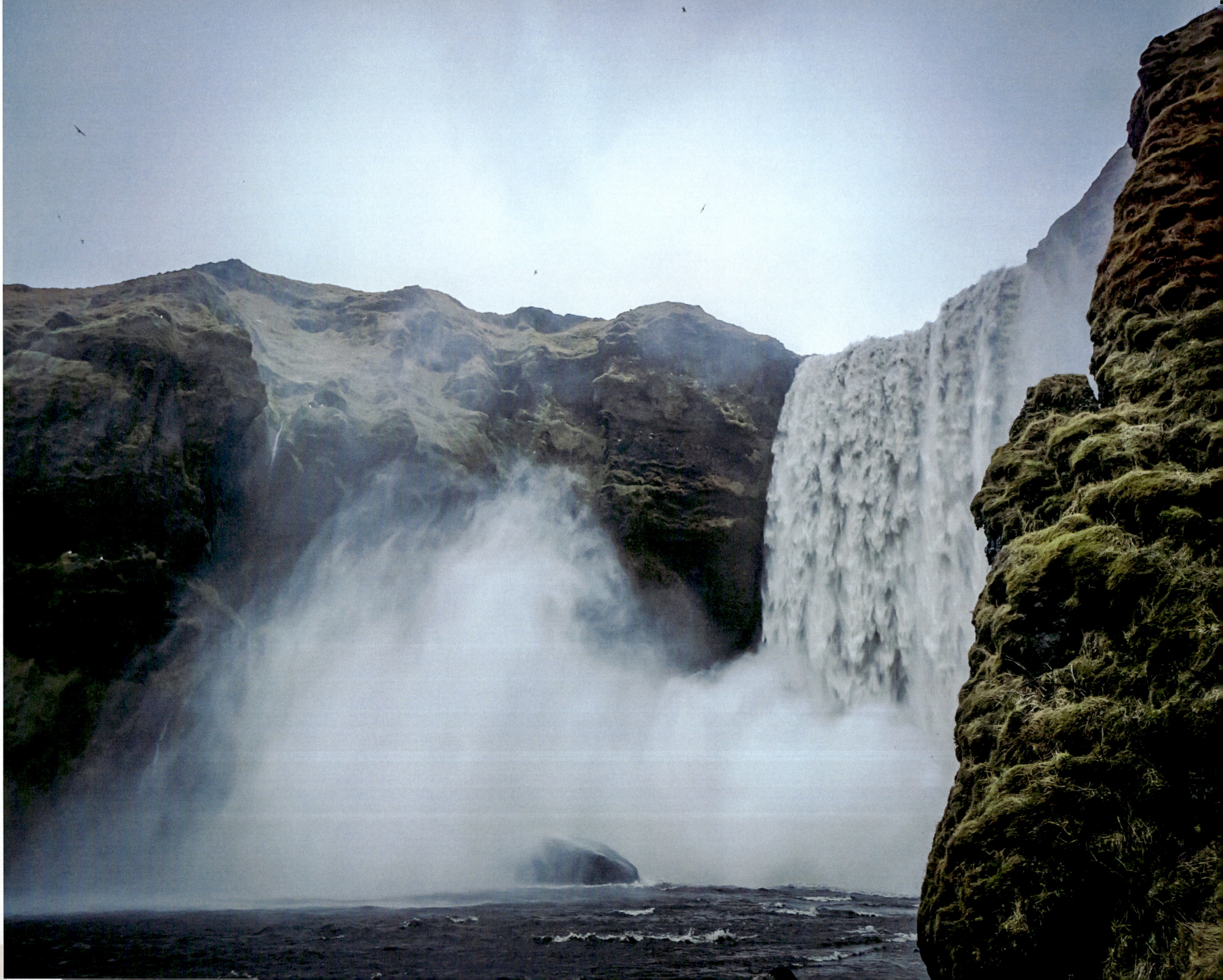

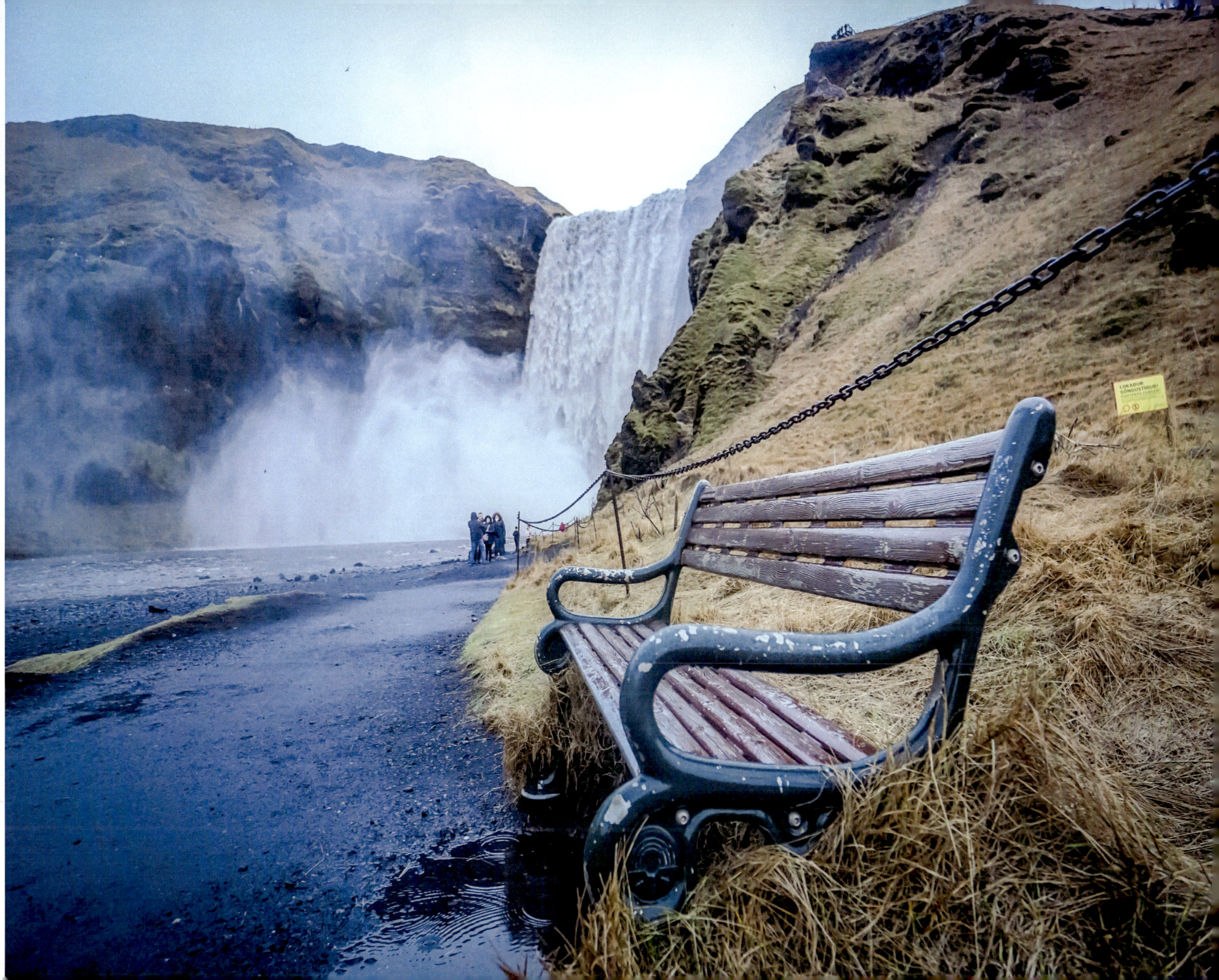
LOKADUR
GÖNGUSTÍGUR!
FOOTPATH CLOSED!

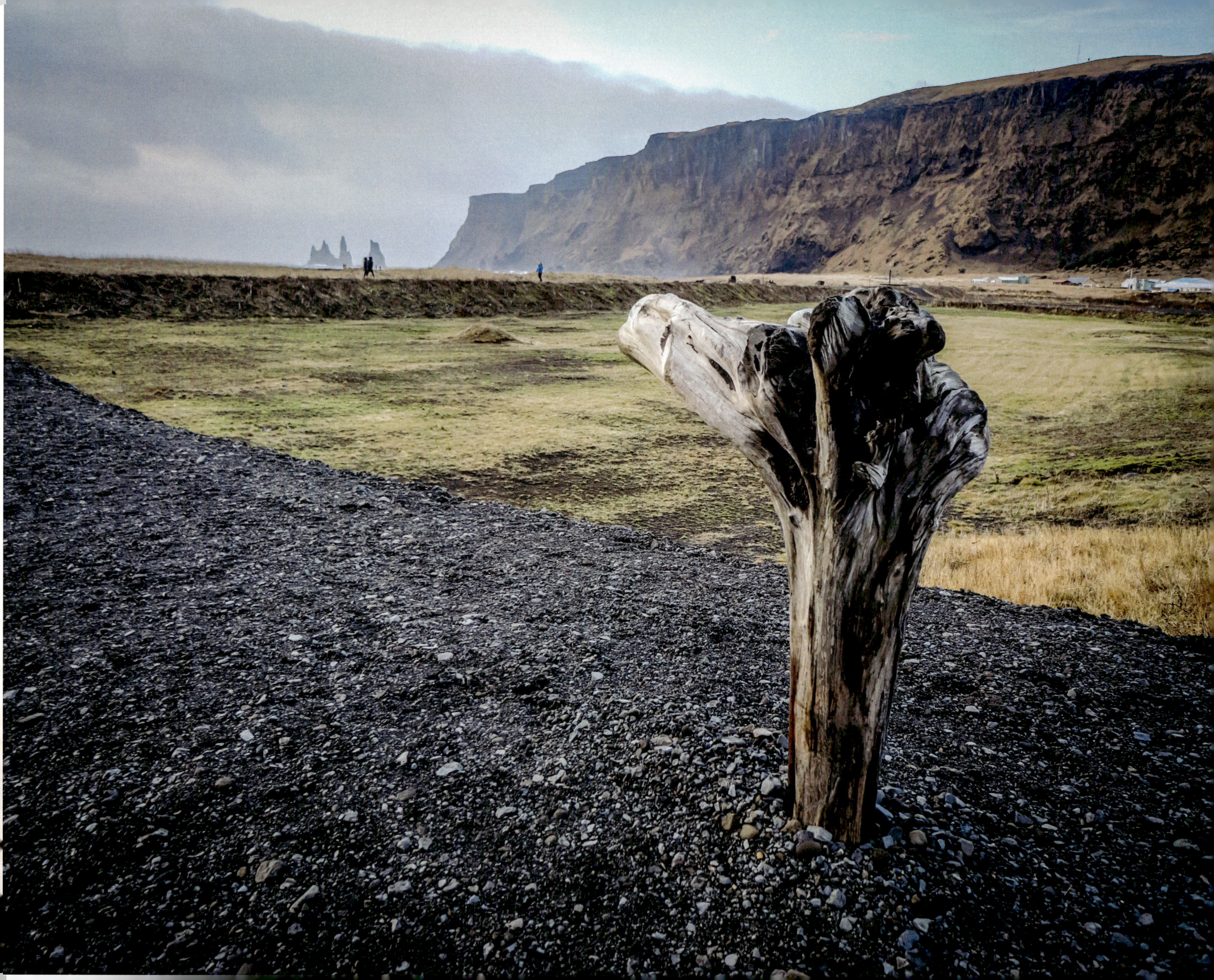

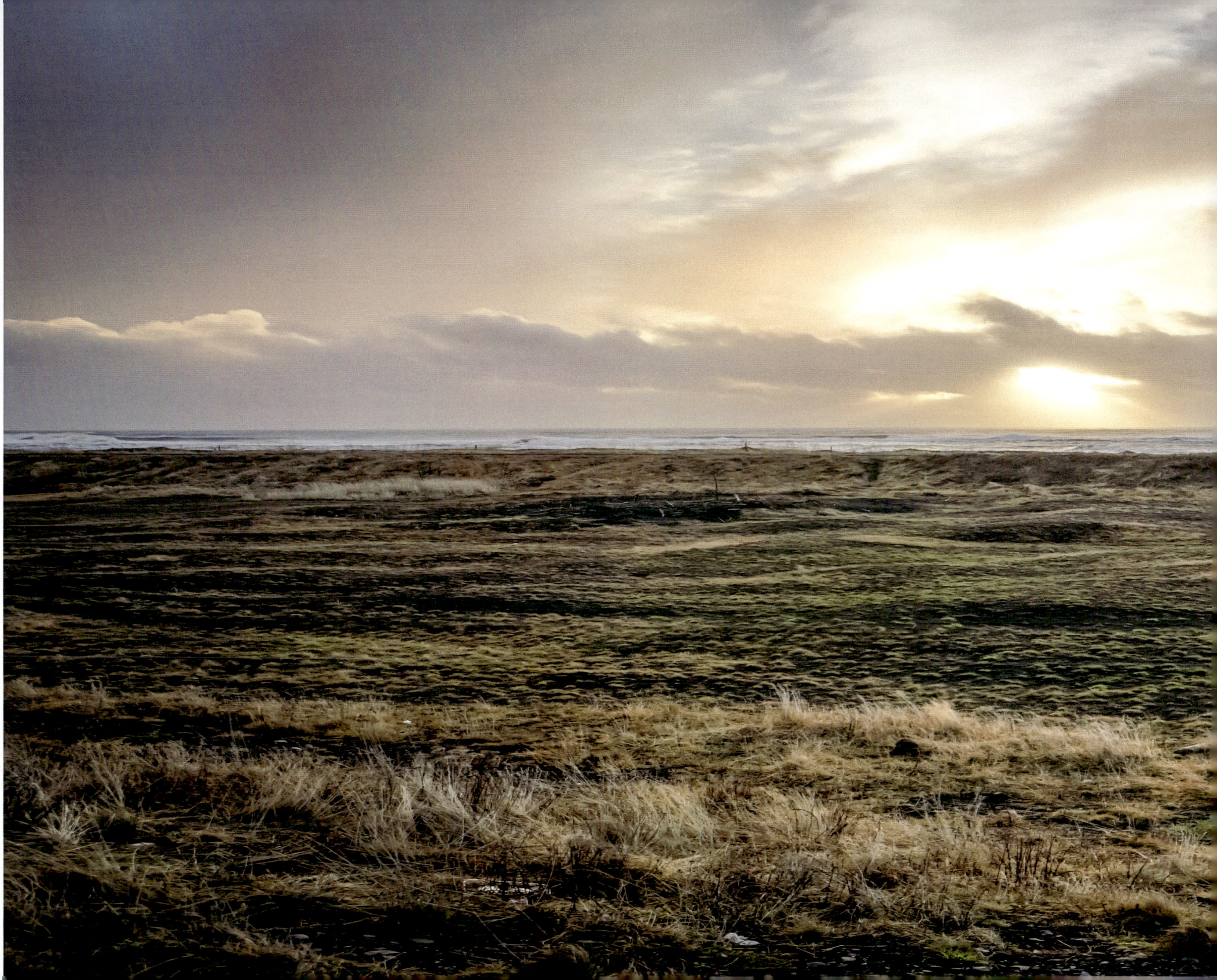

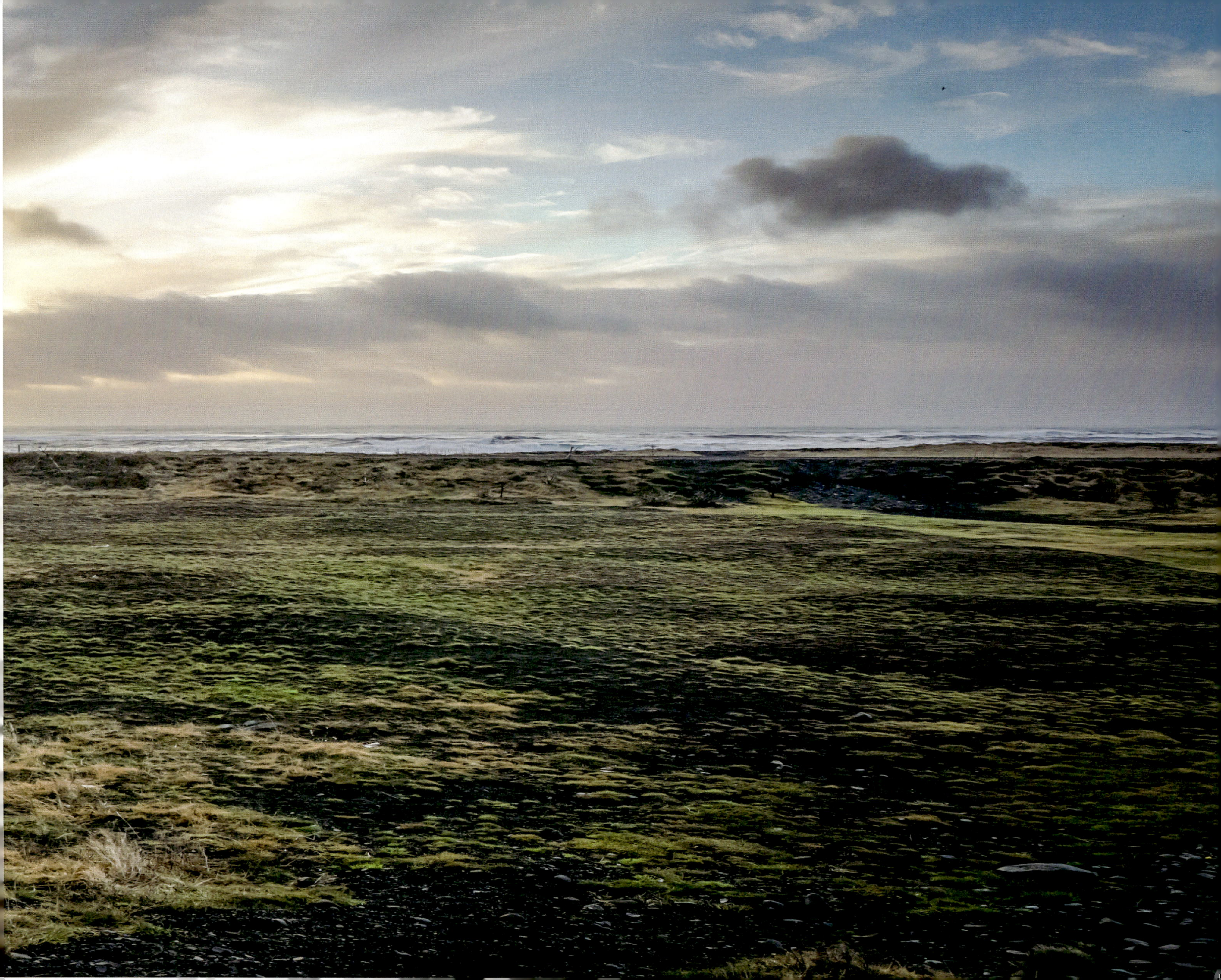

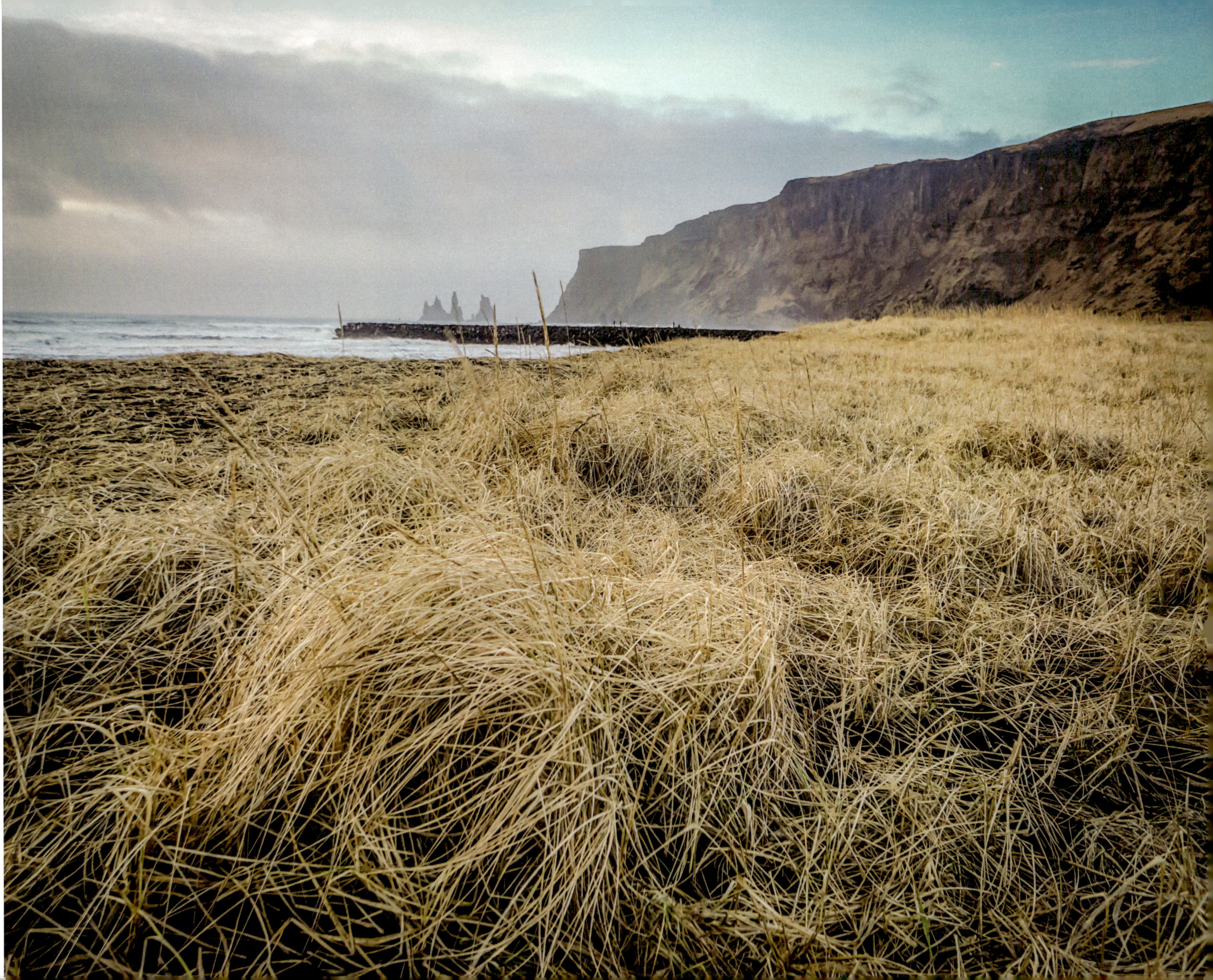

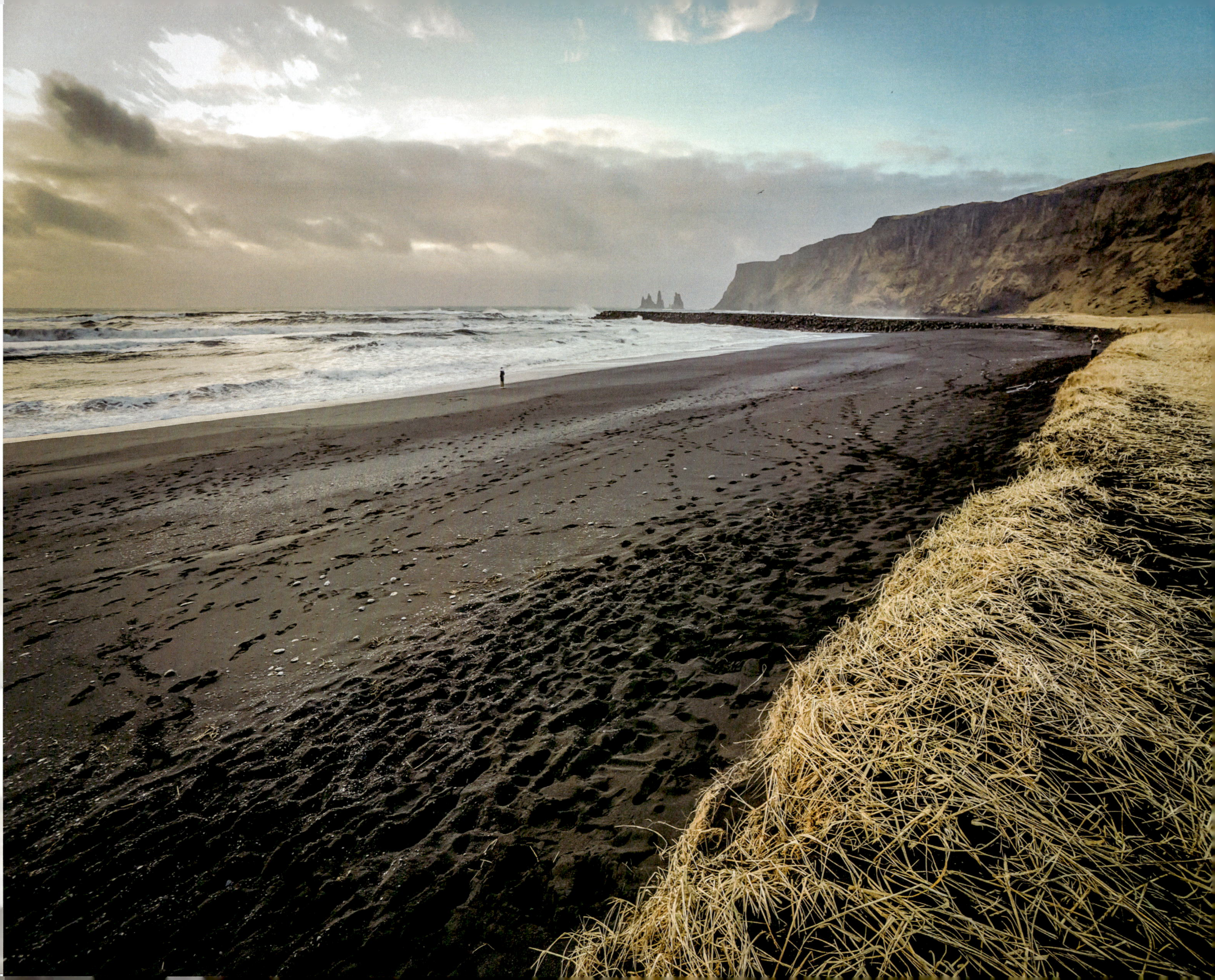

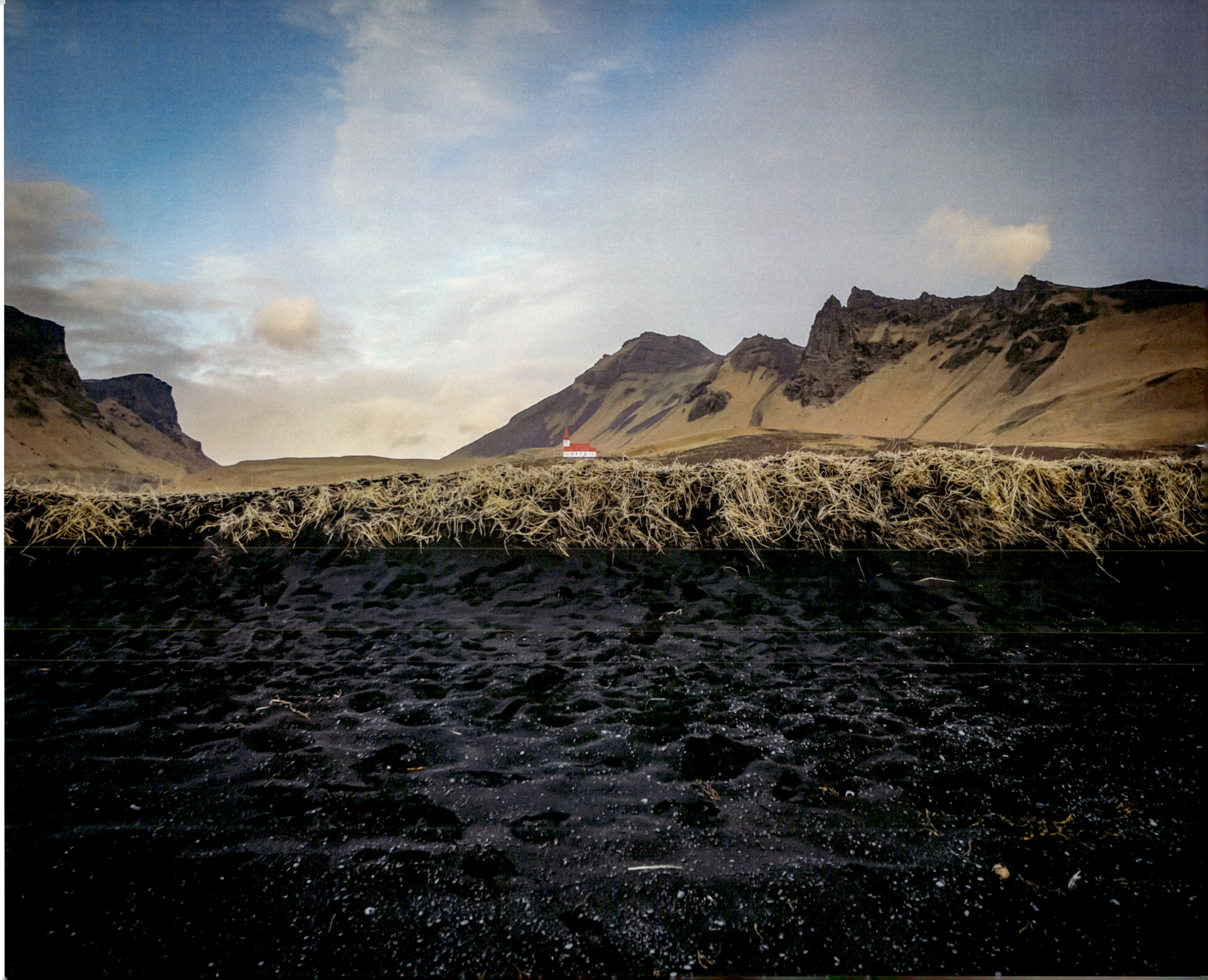

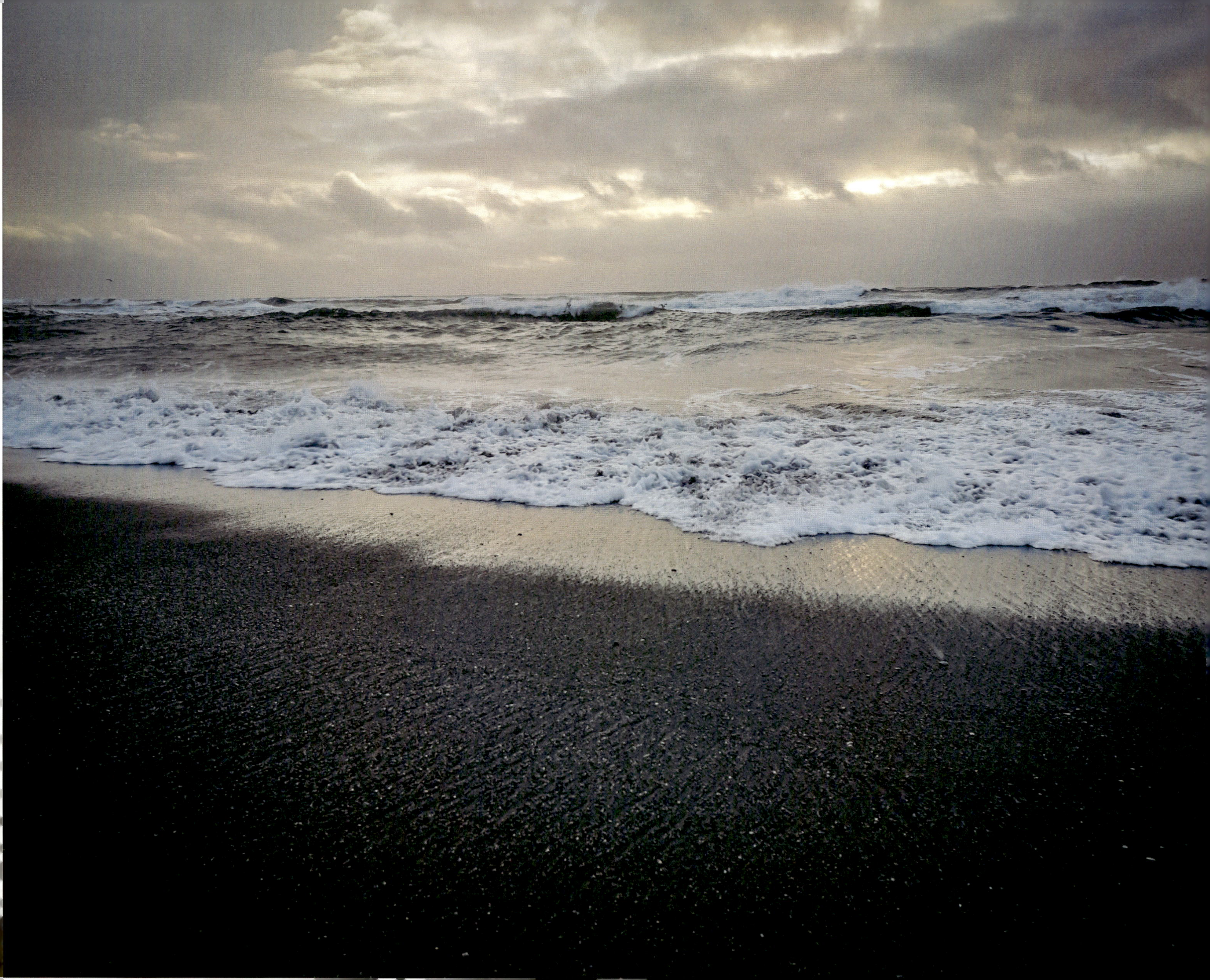

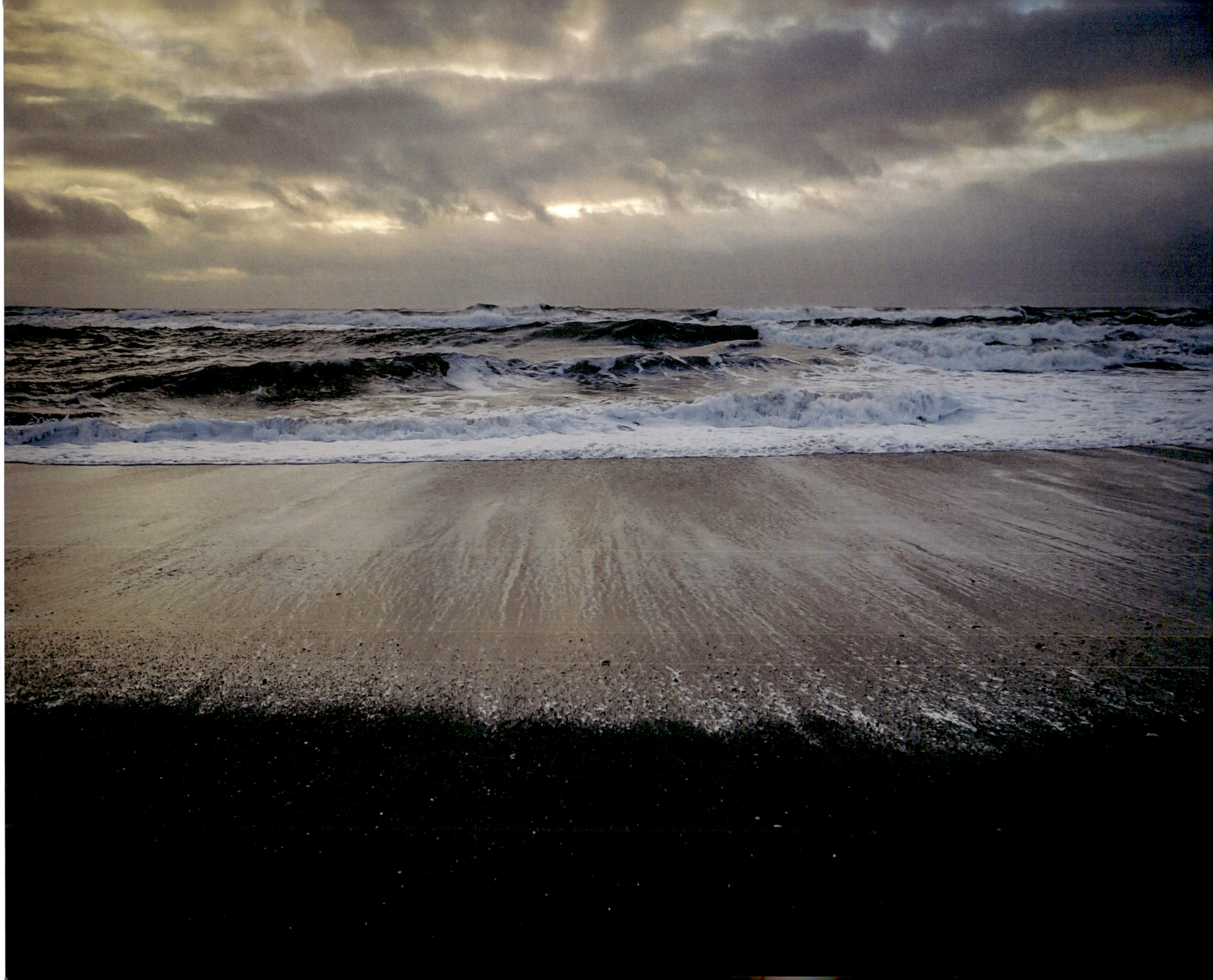

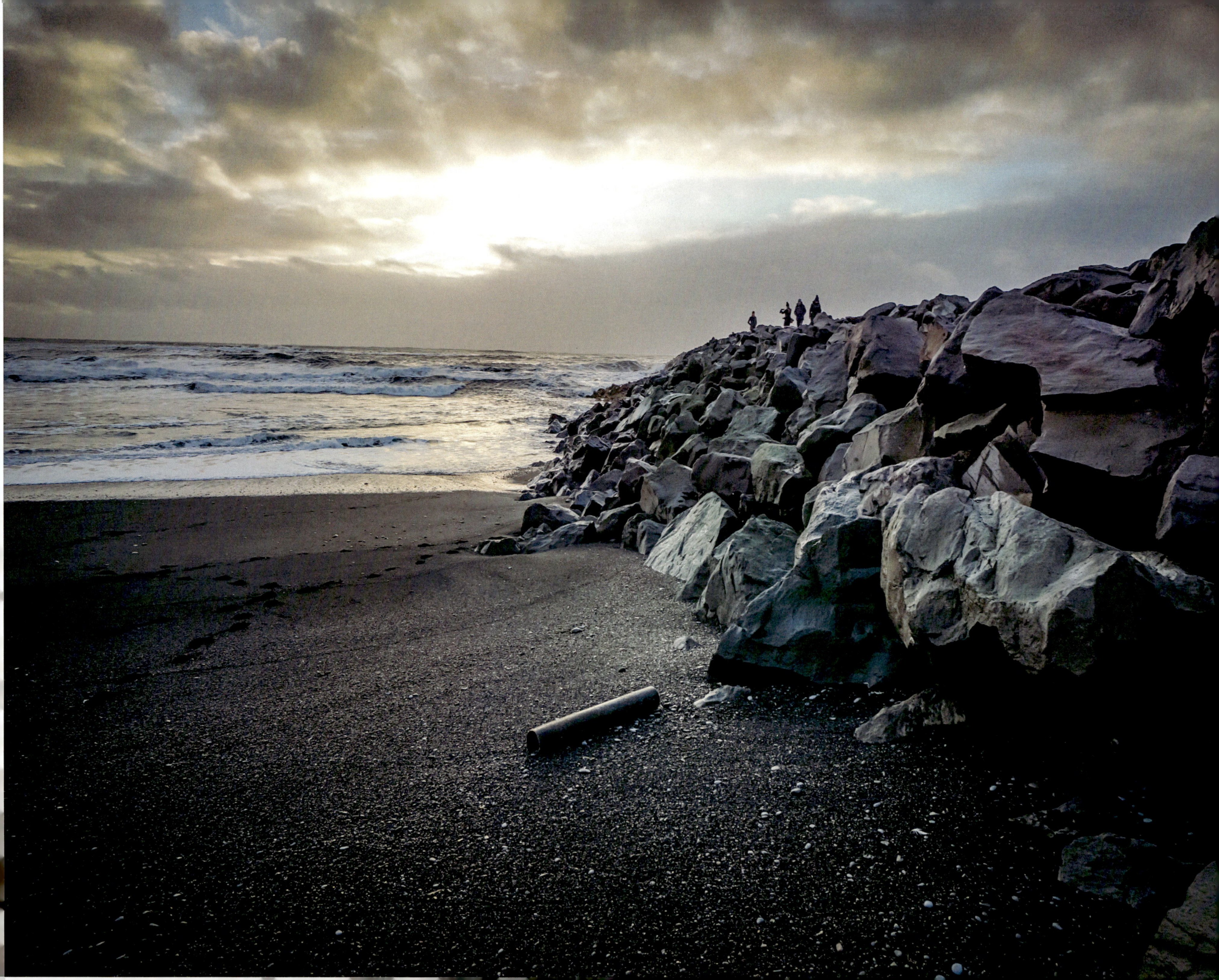

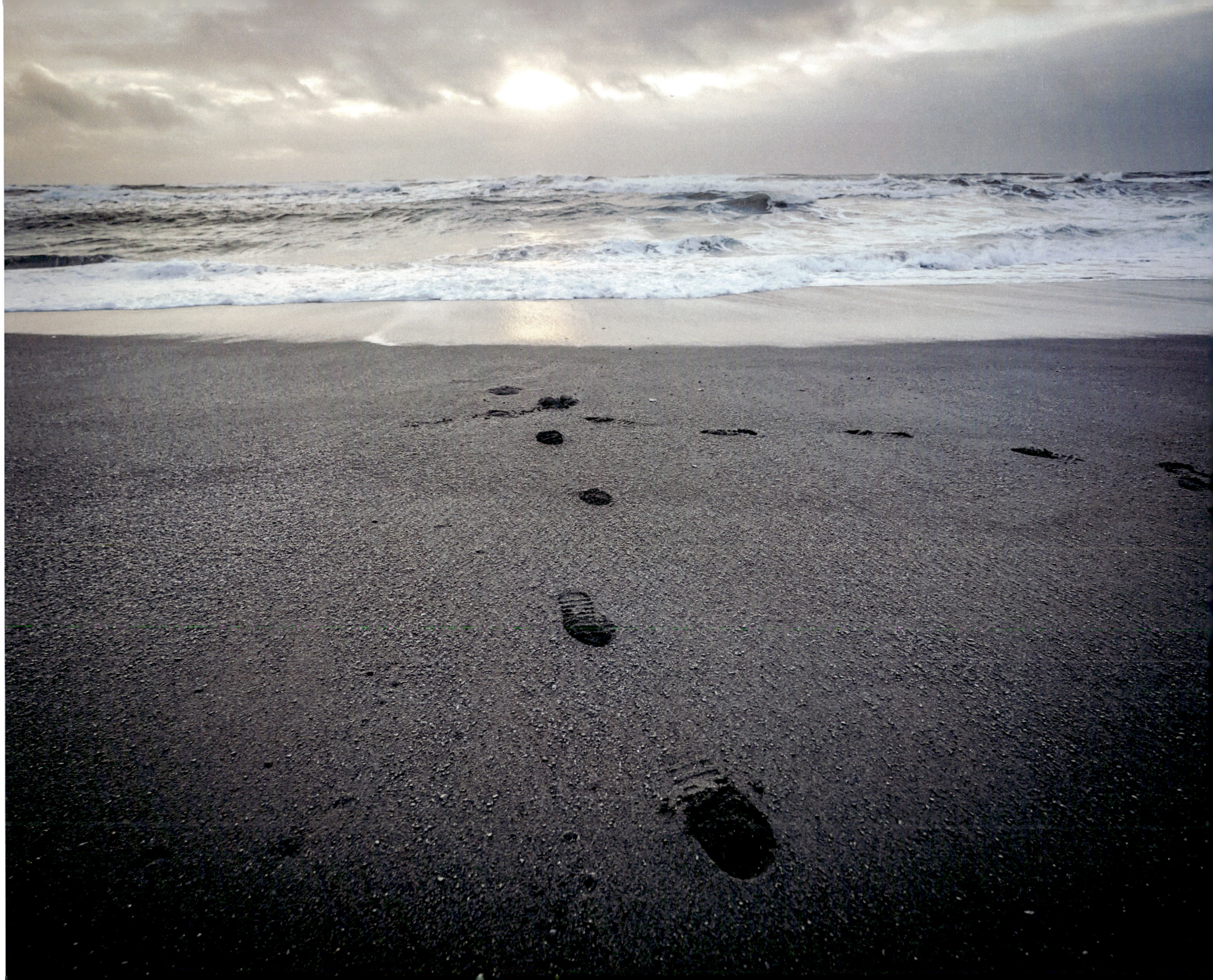

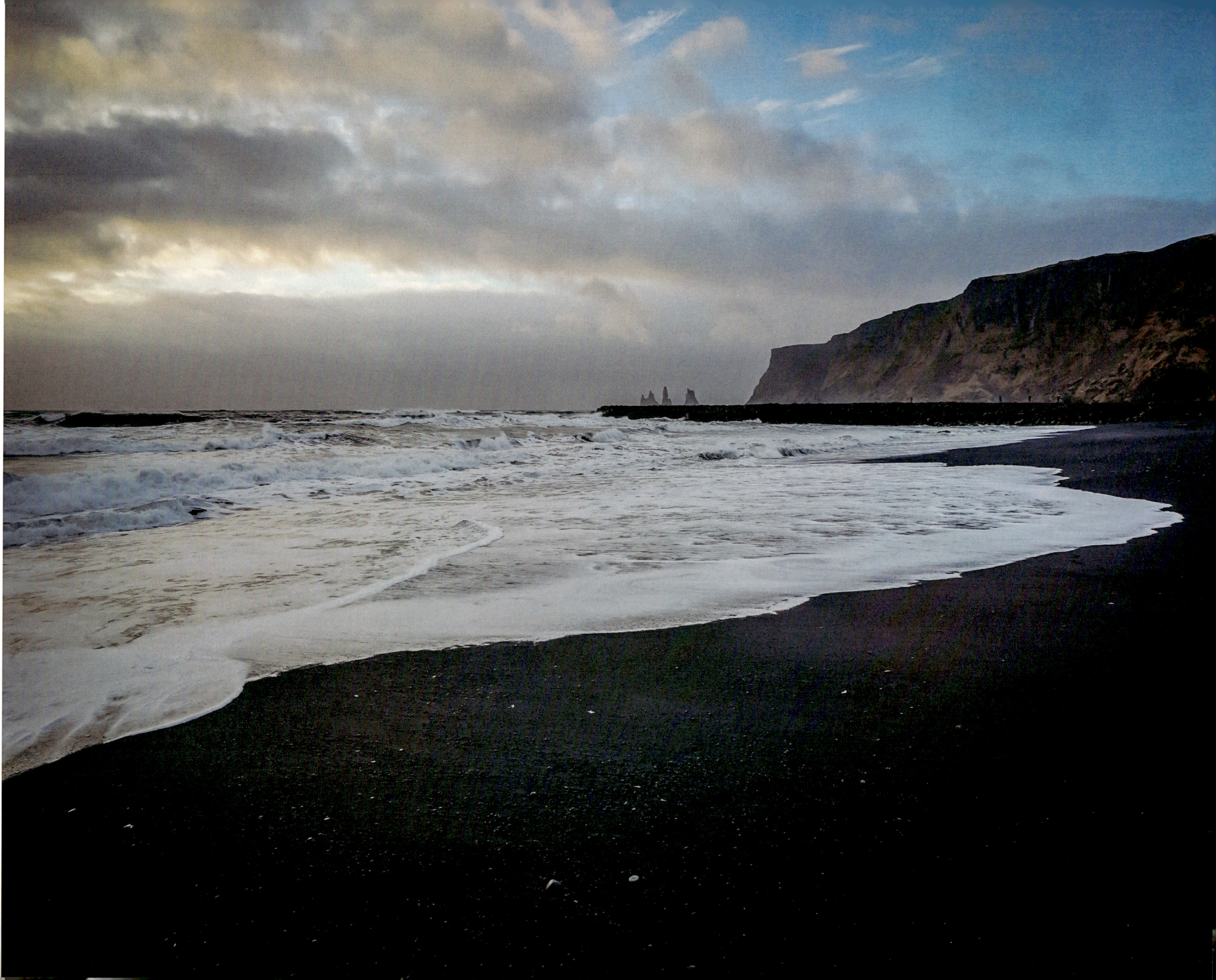

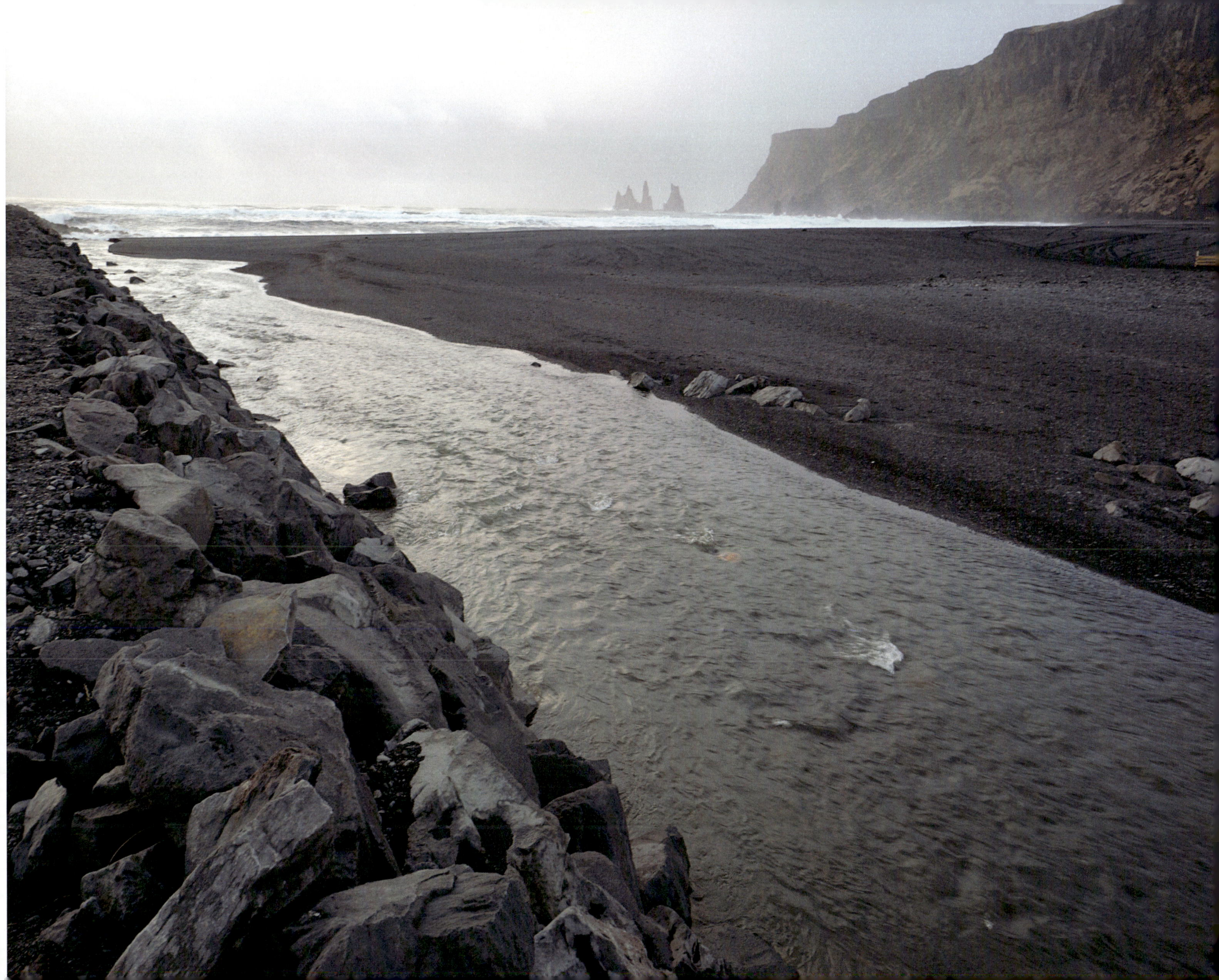

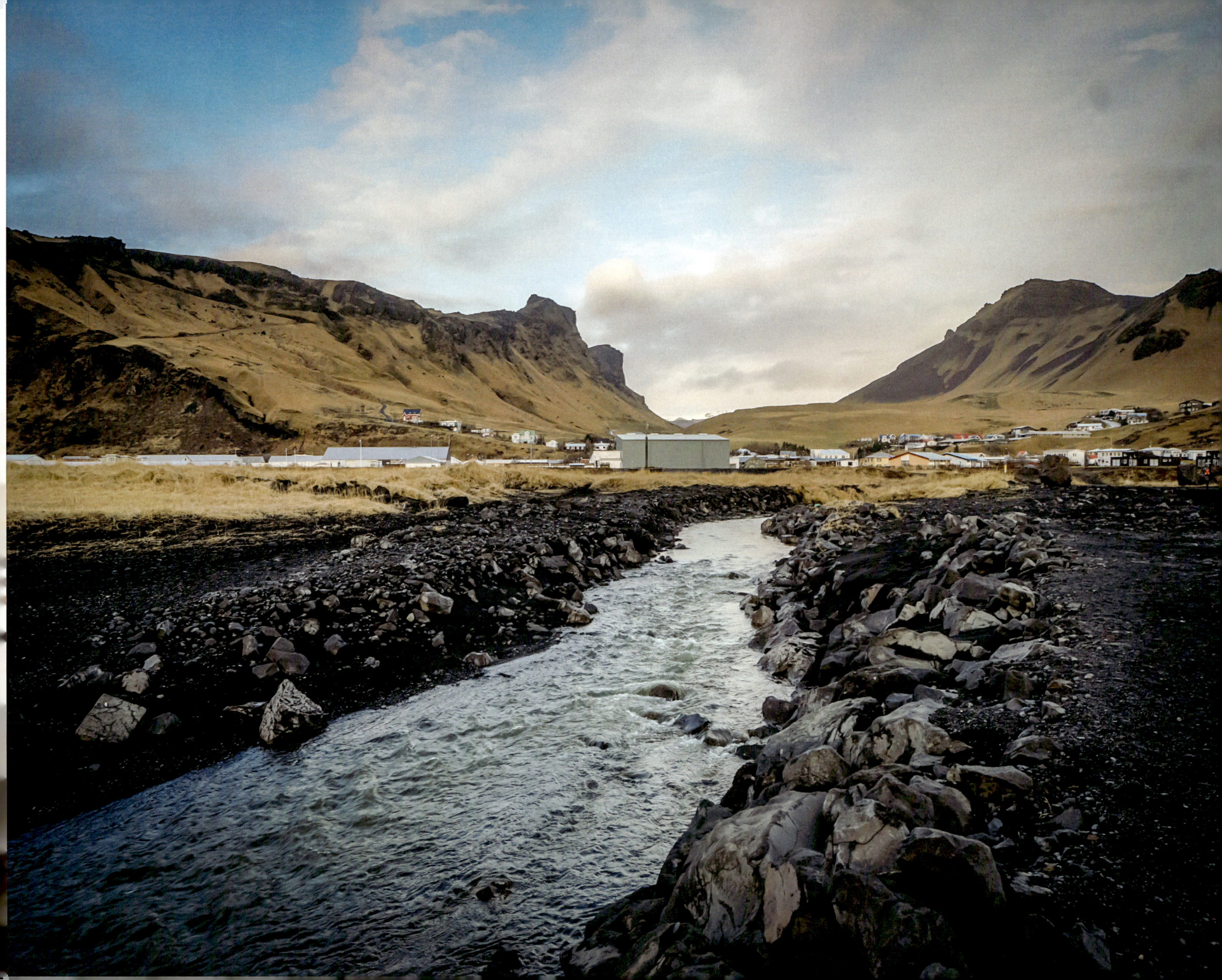

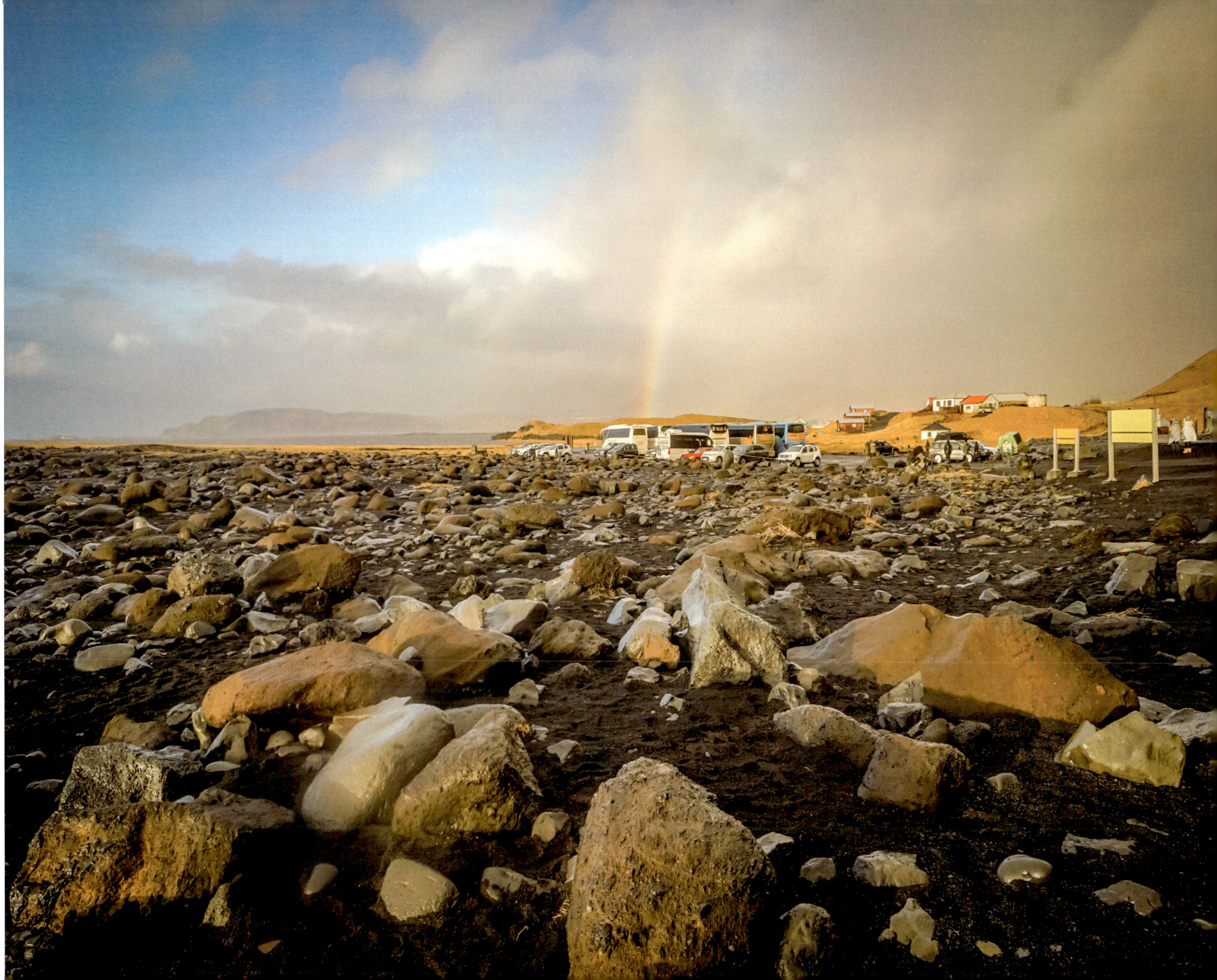

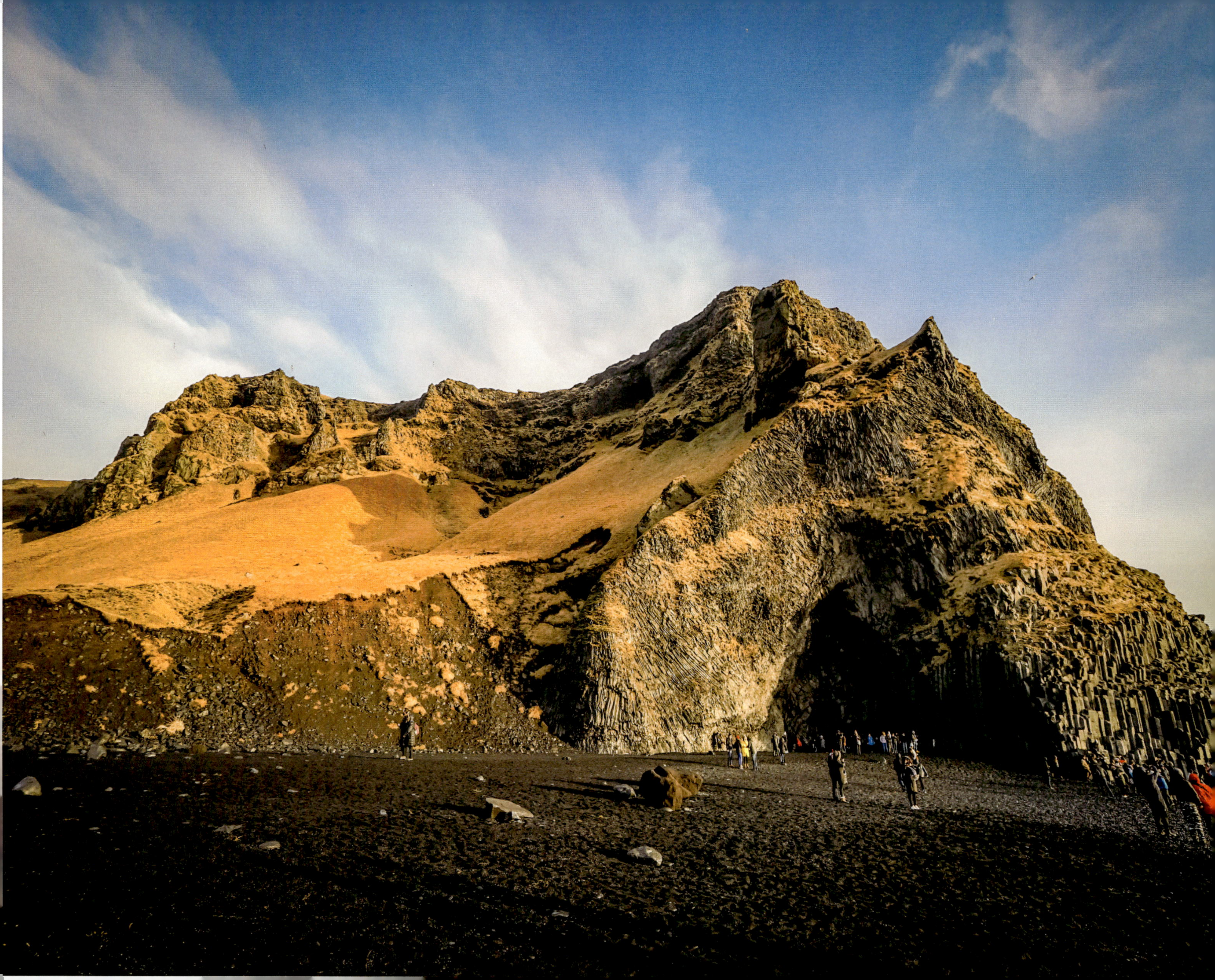

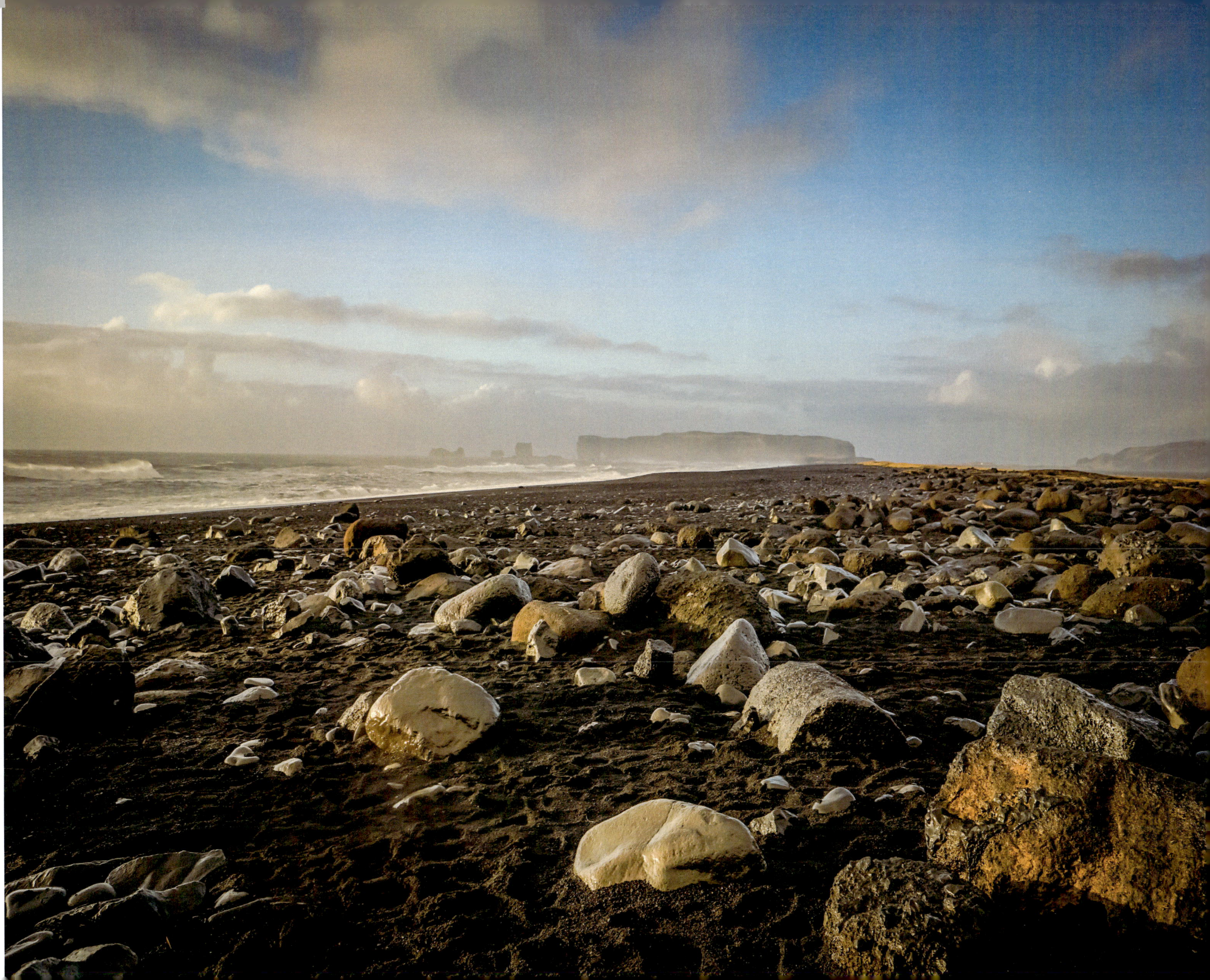

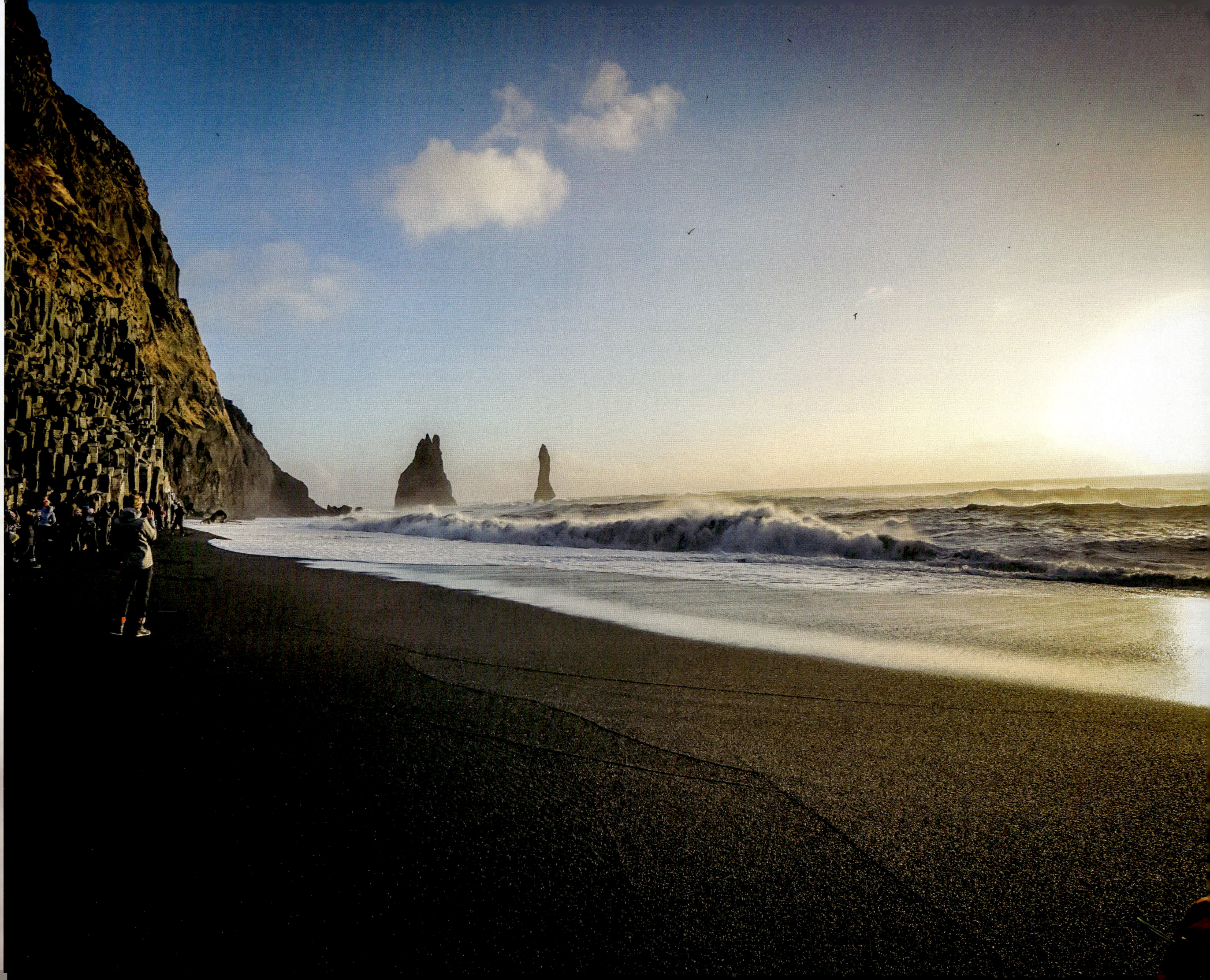

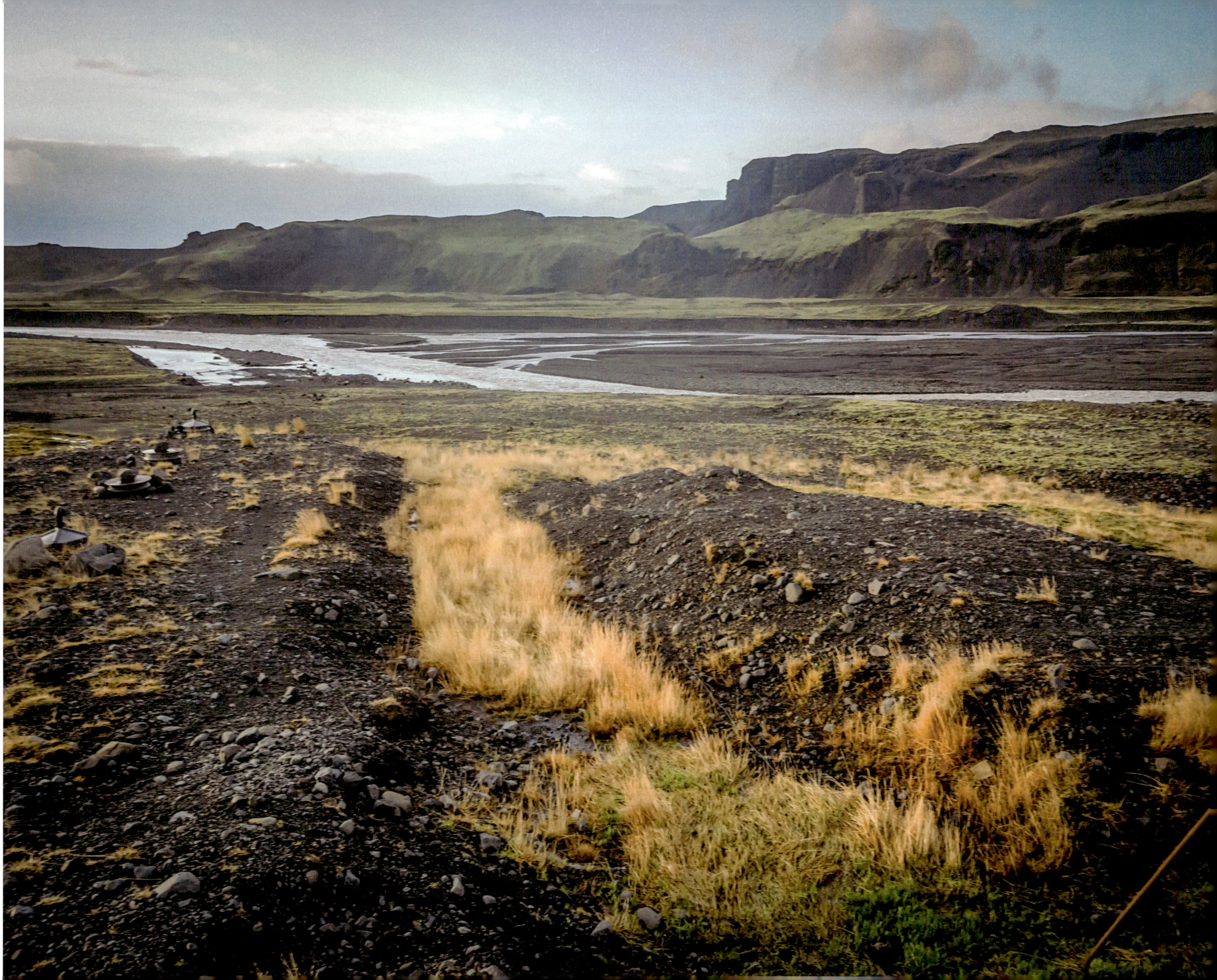

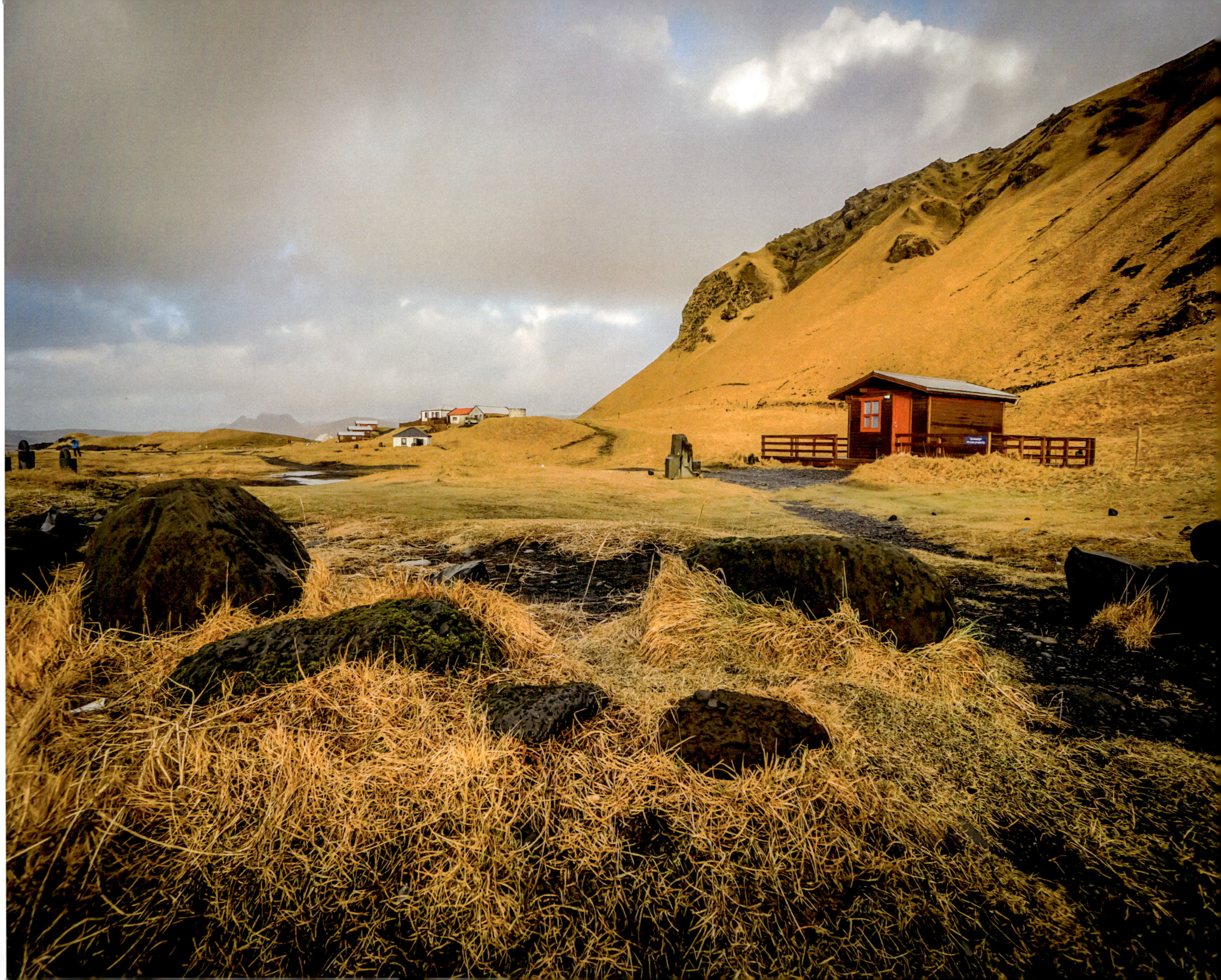

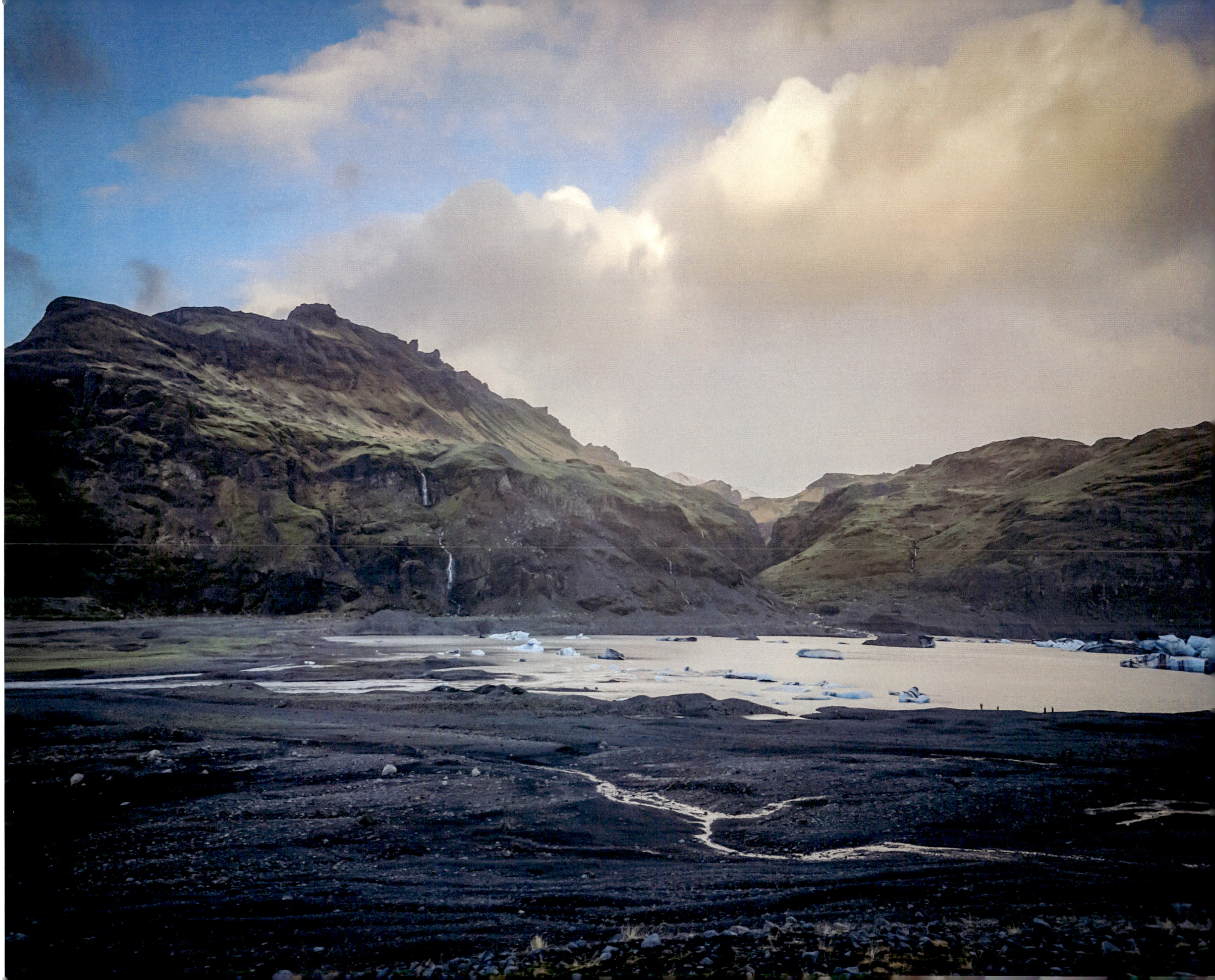

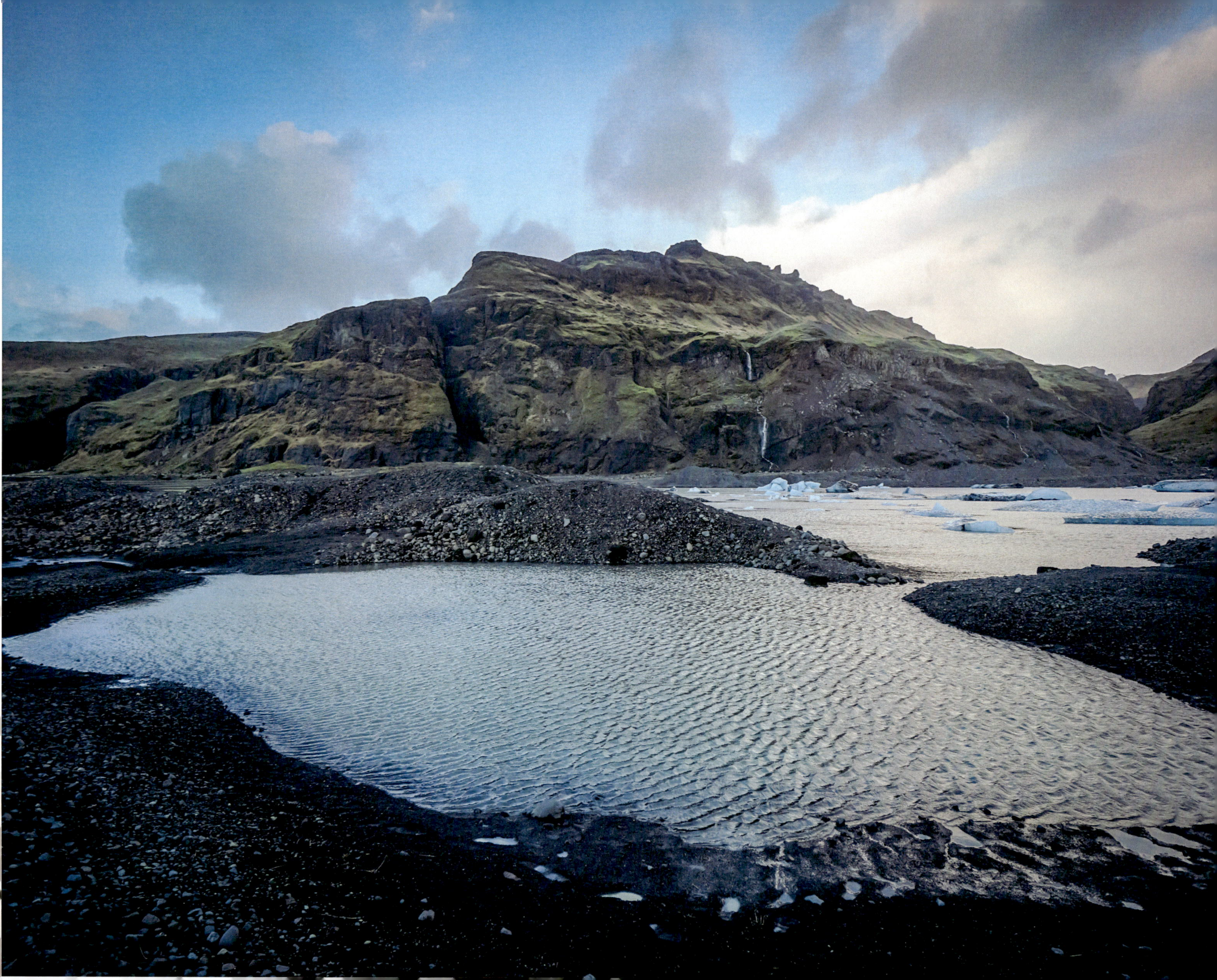

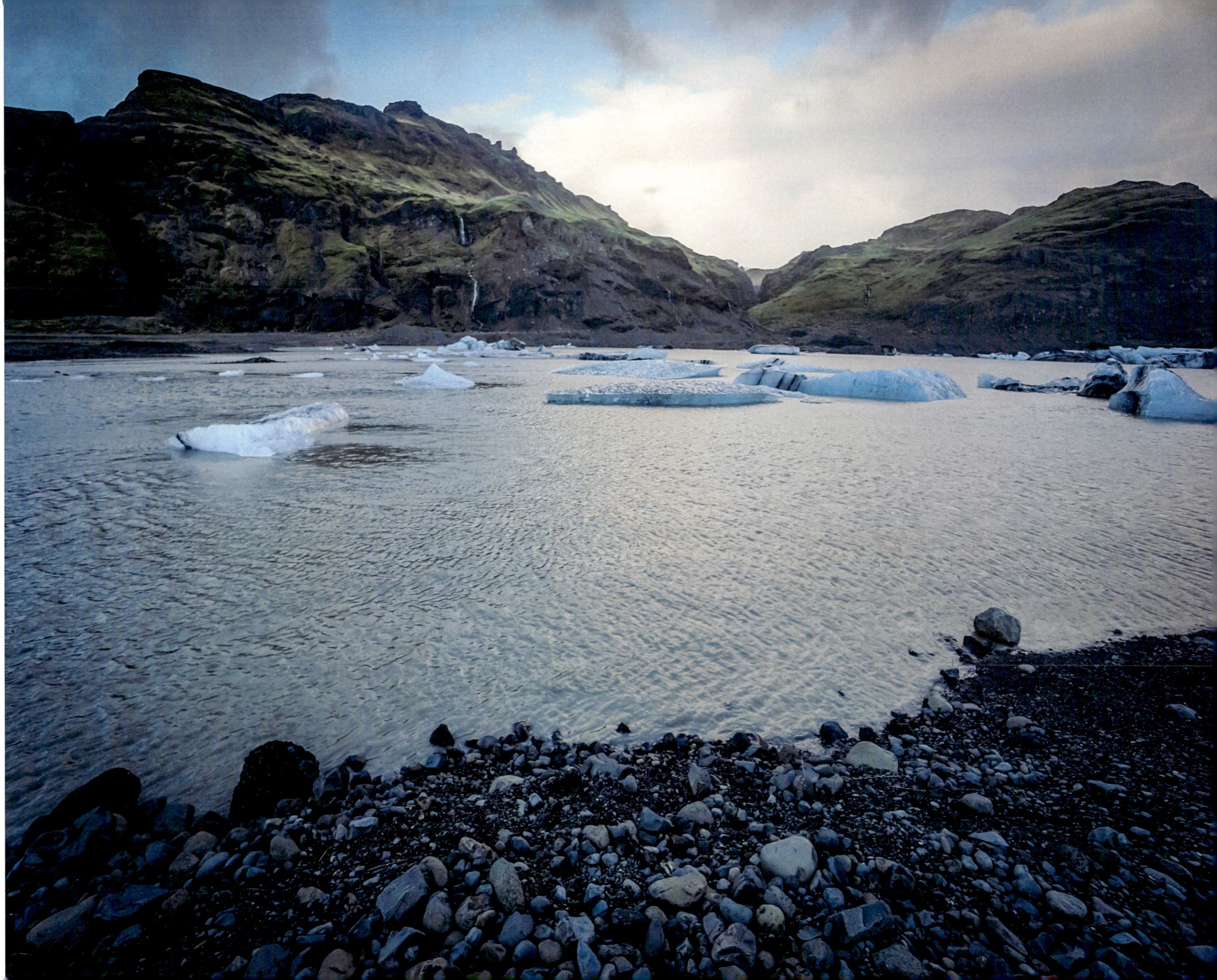

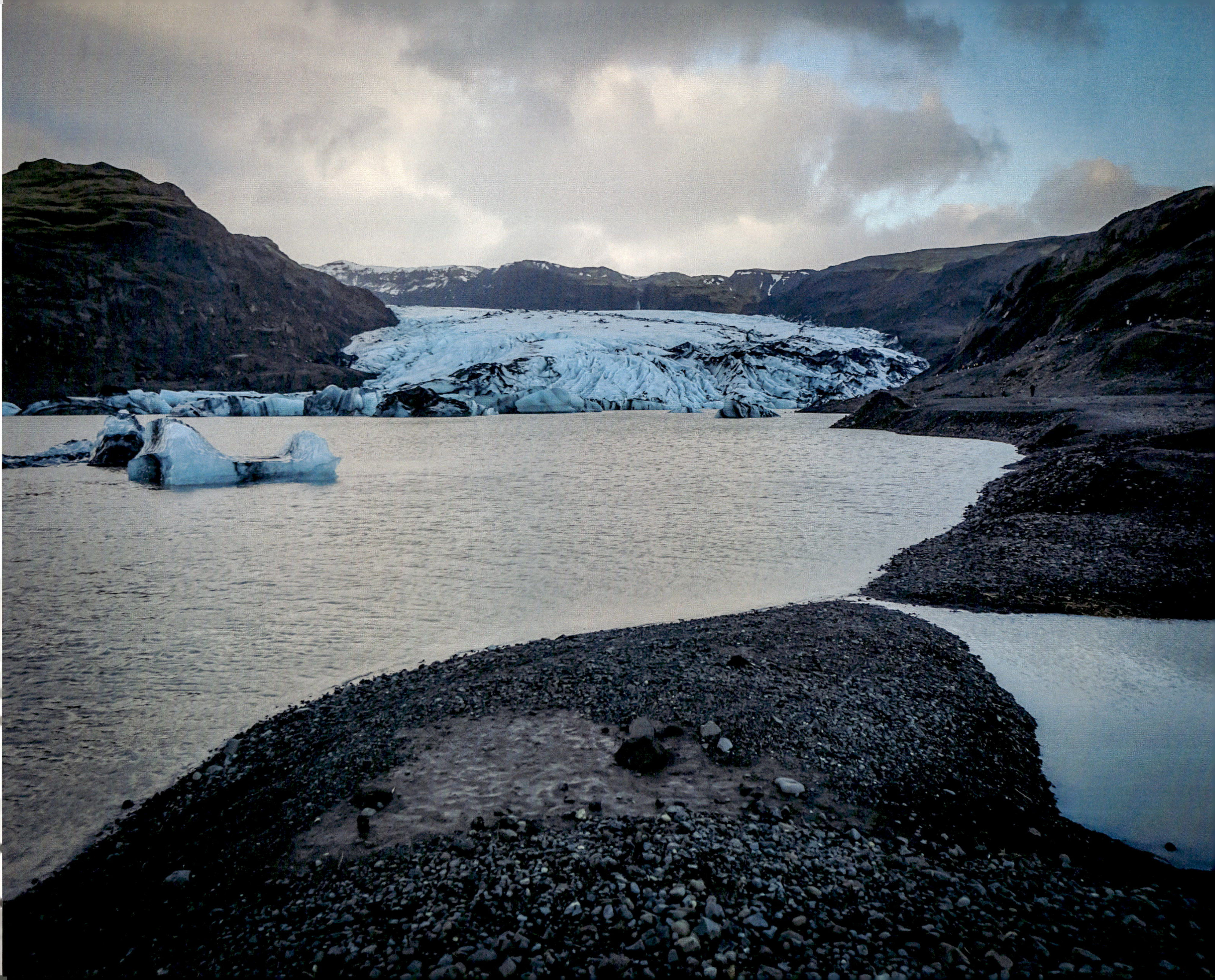

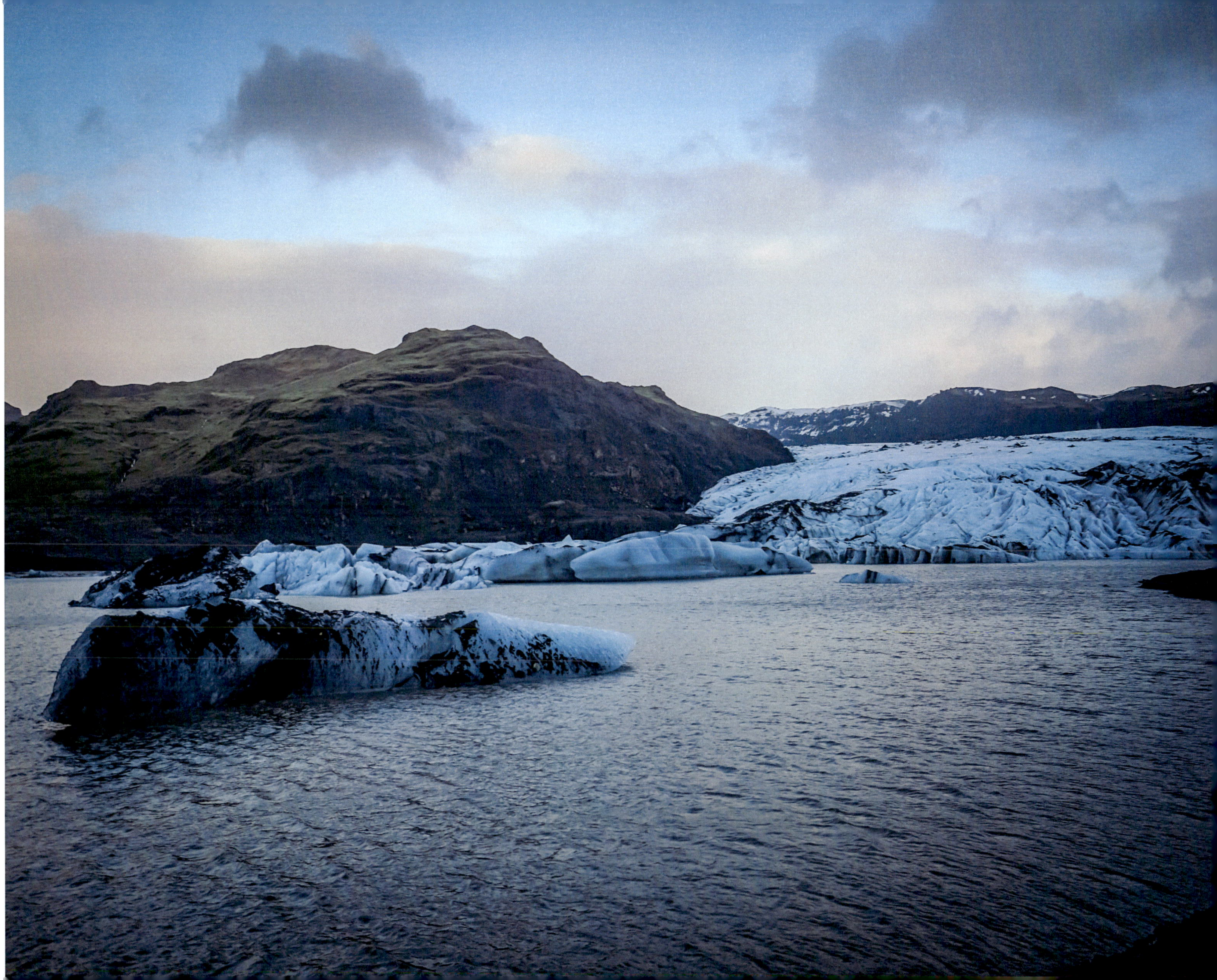

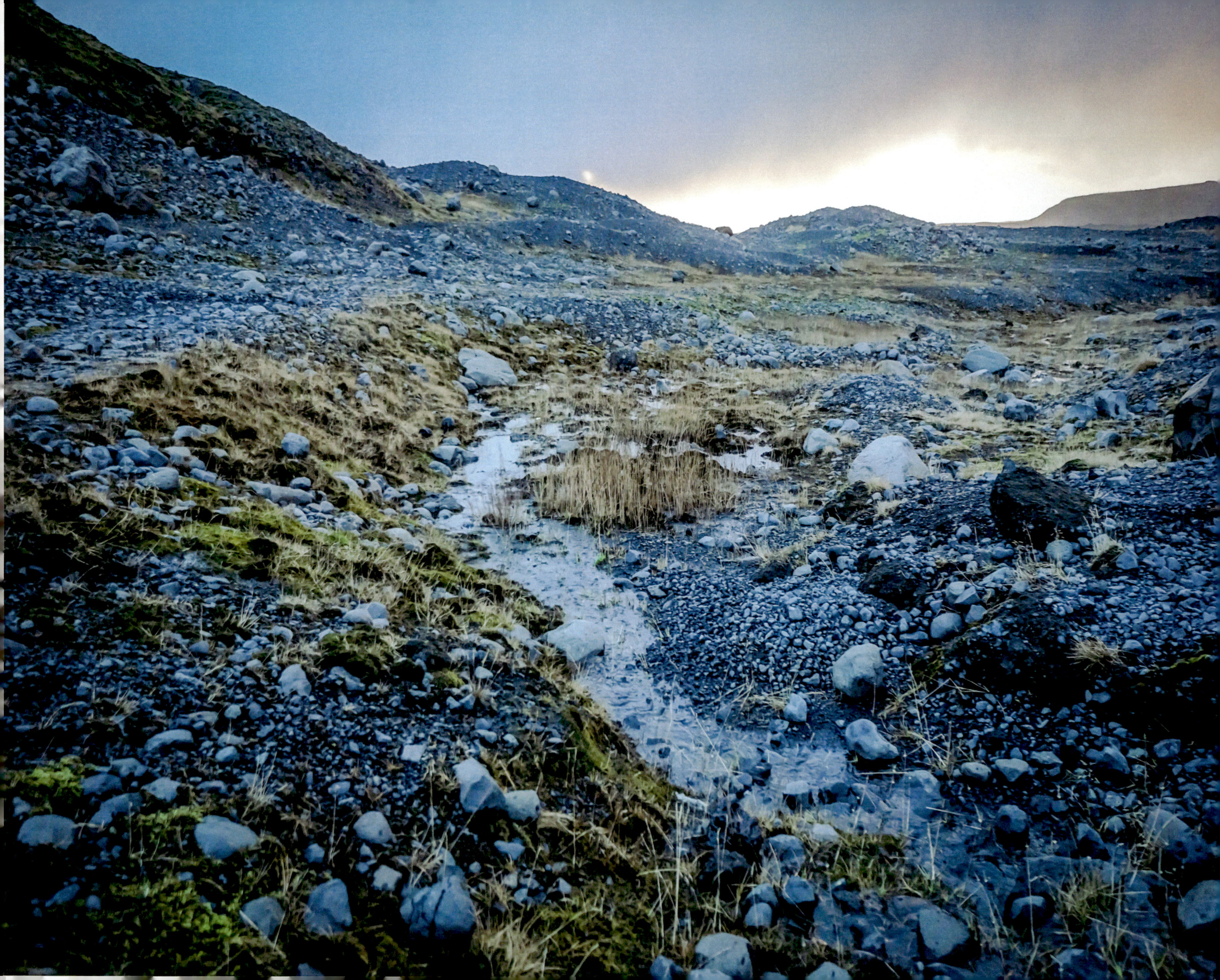

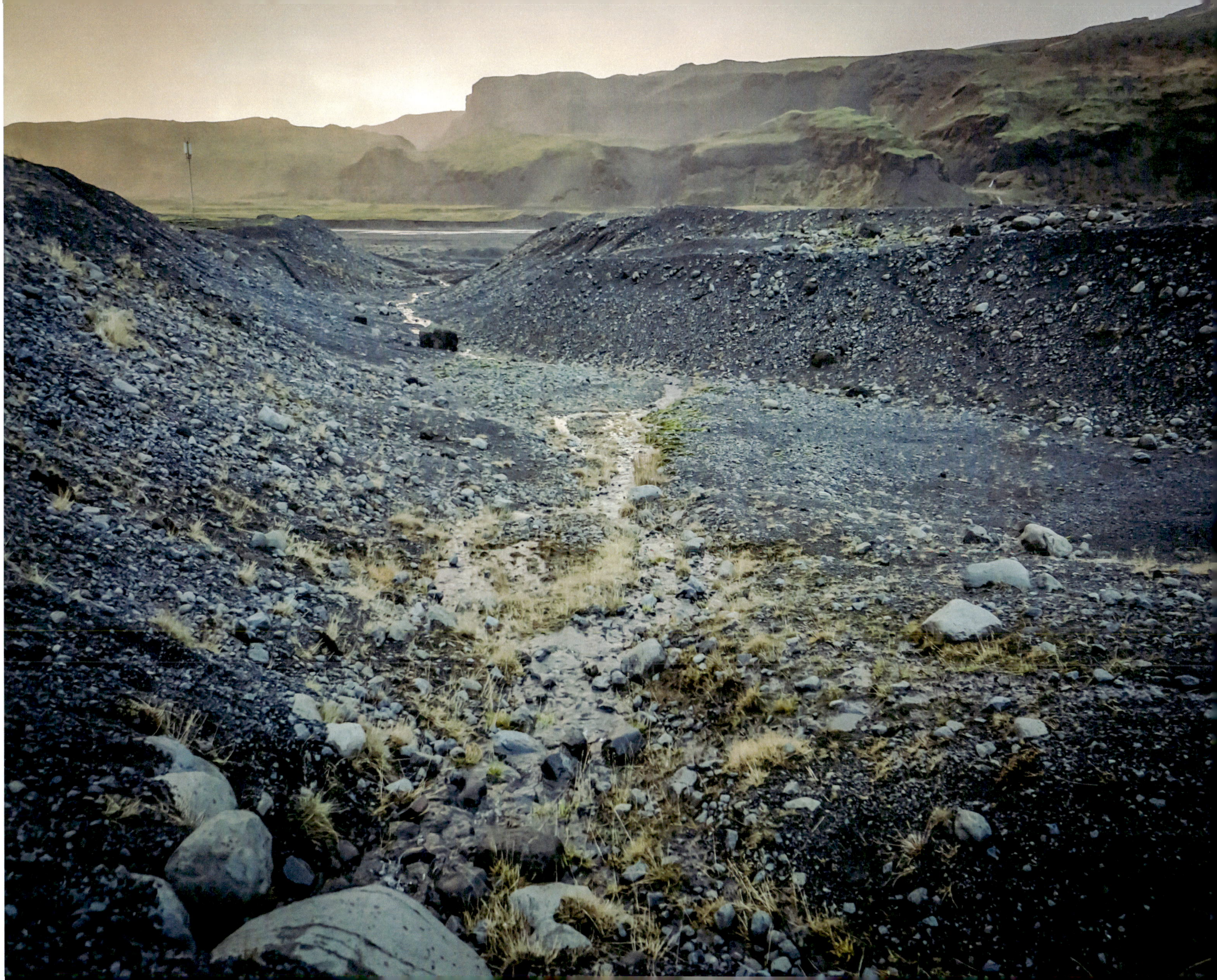

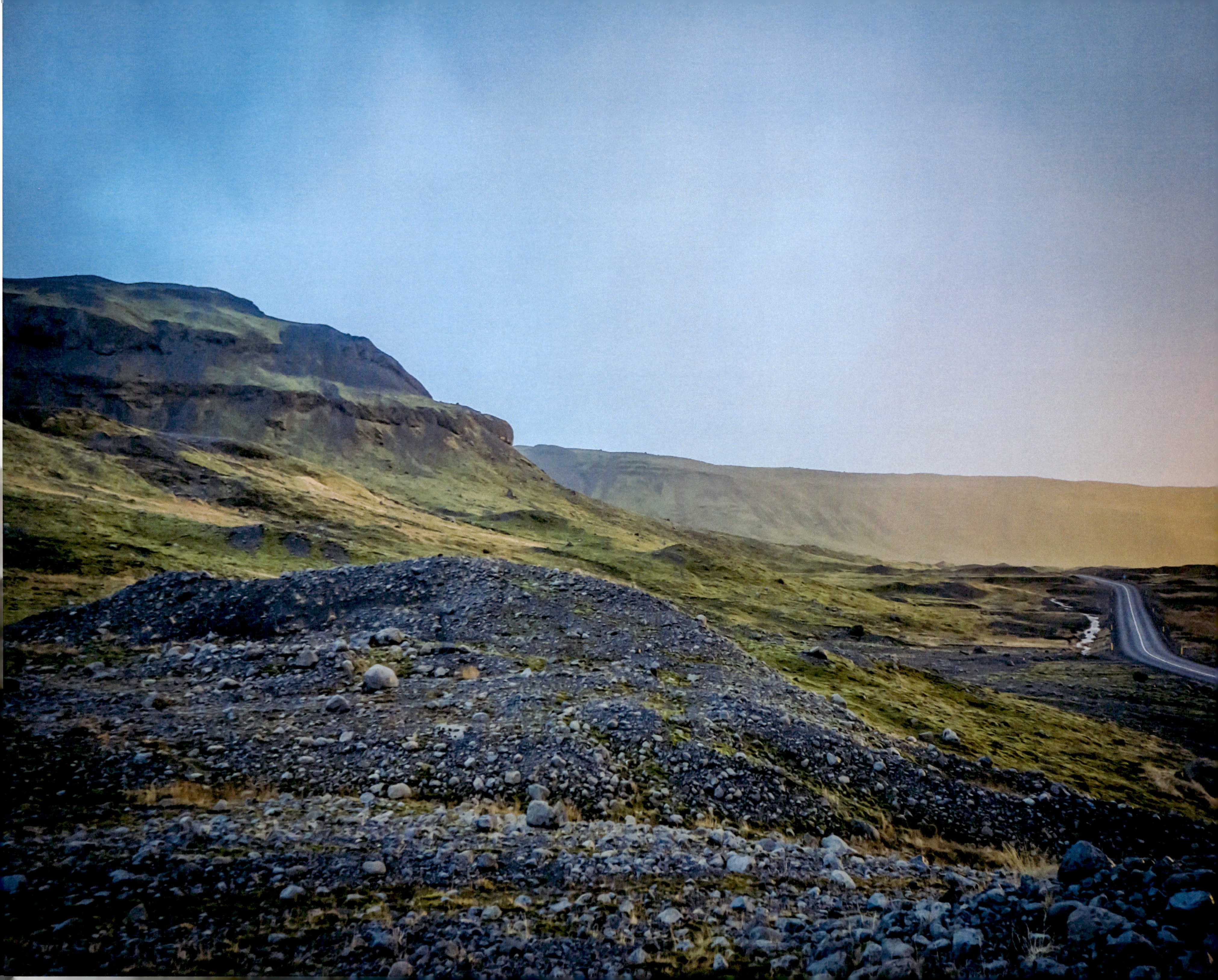

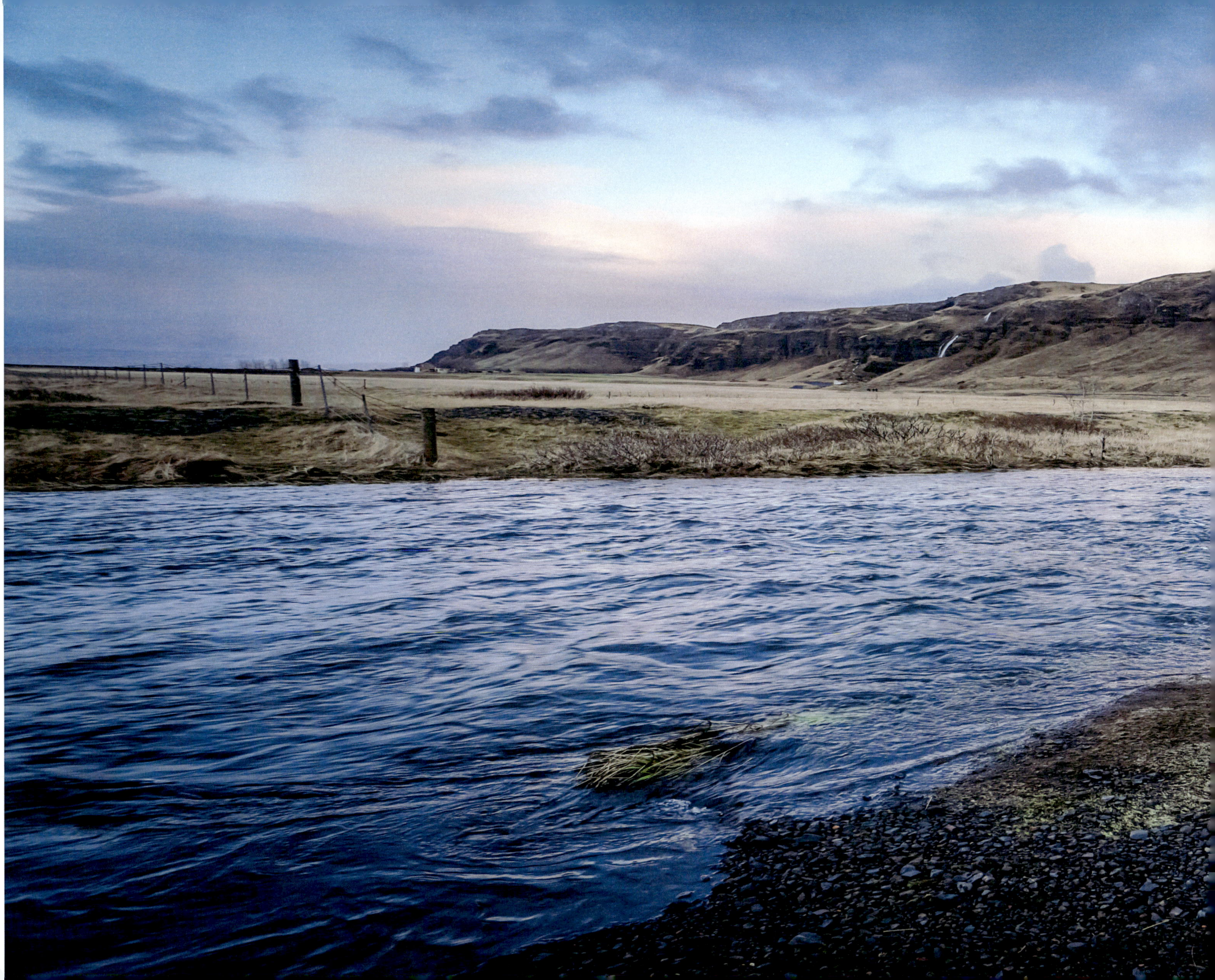

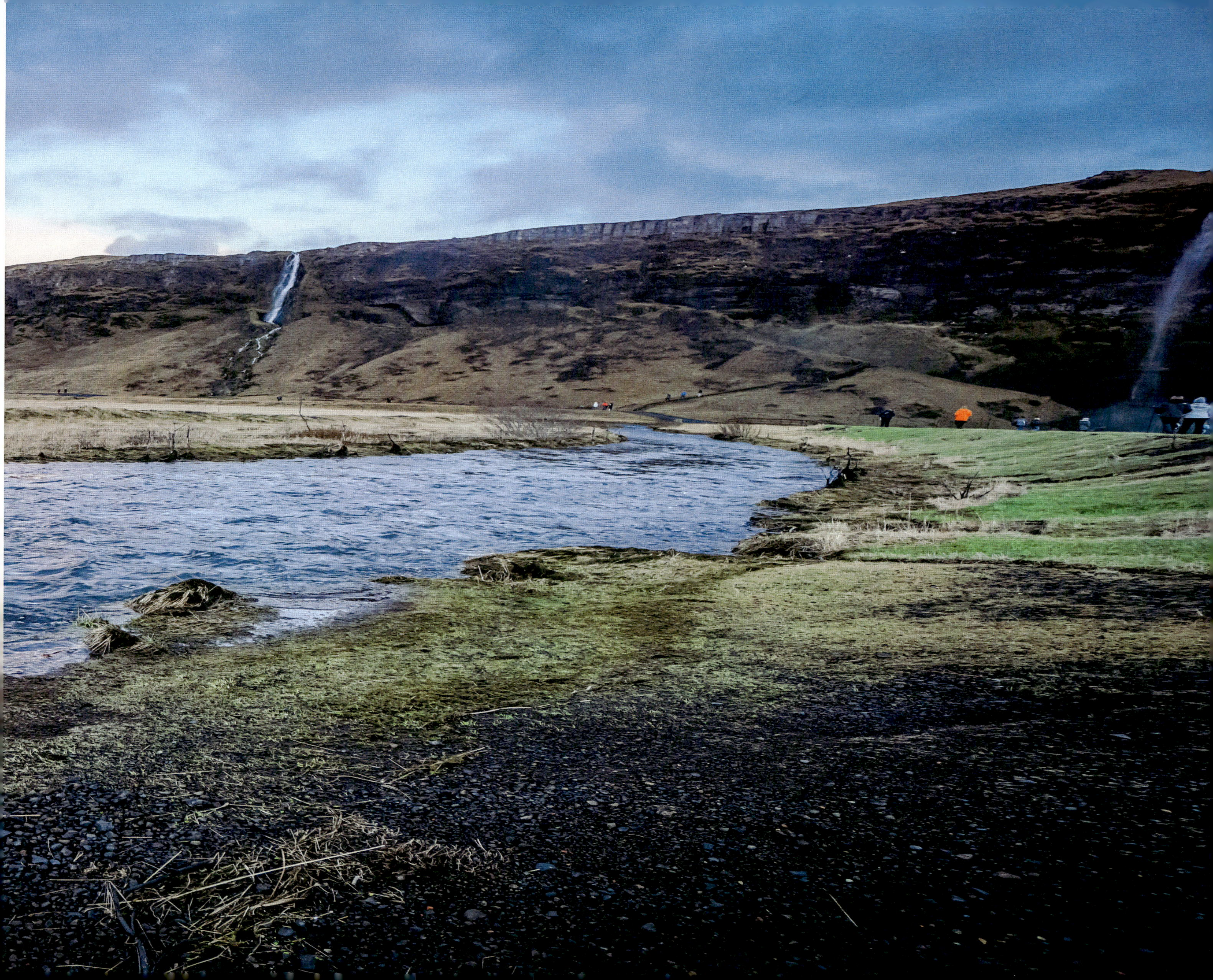

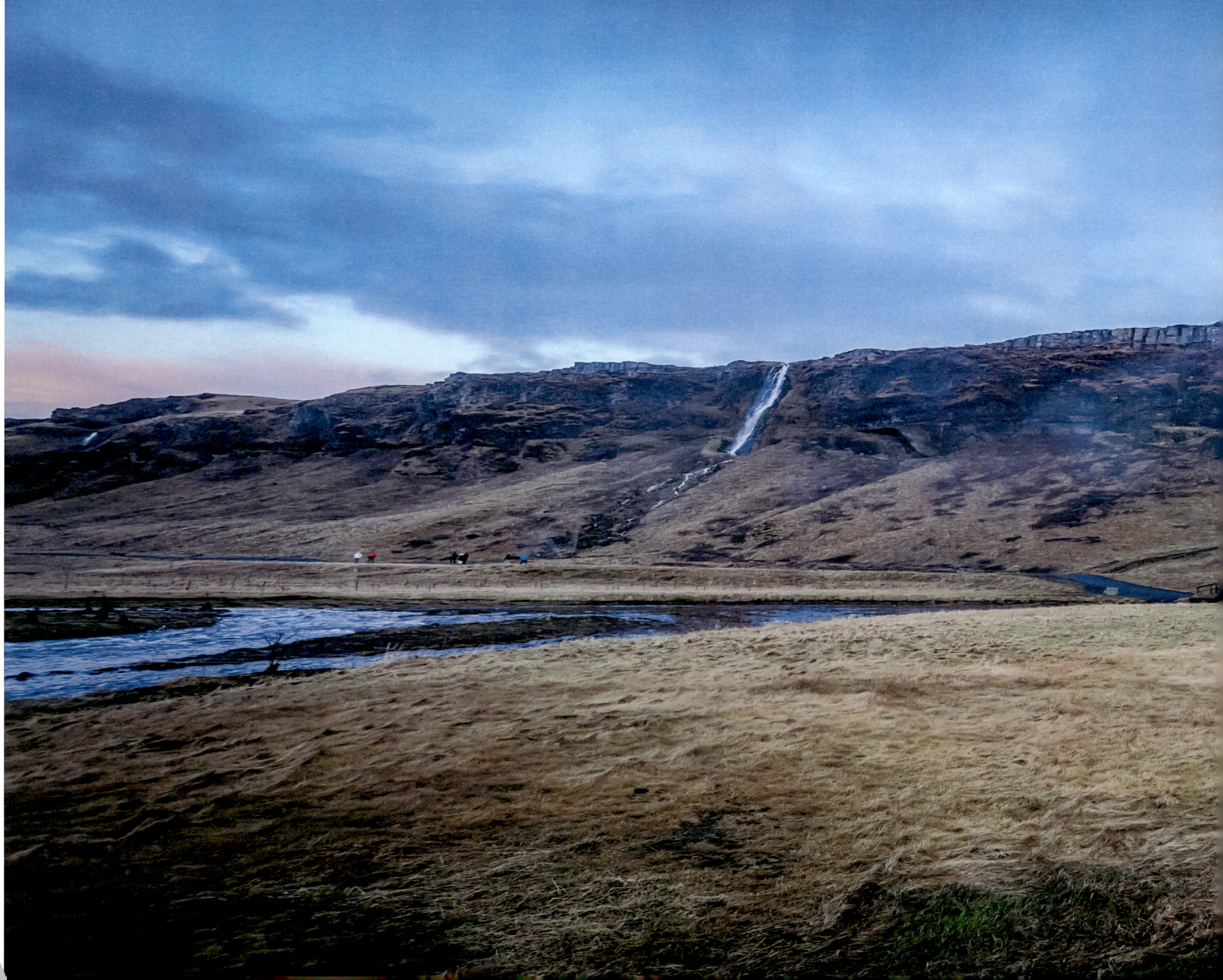

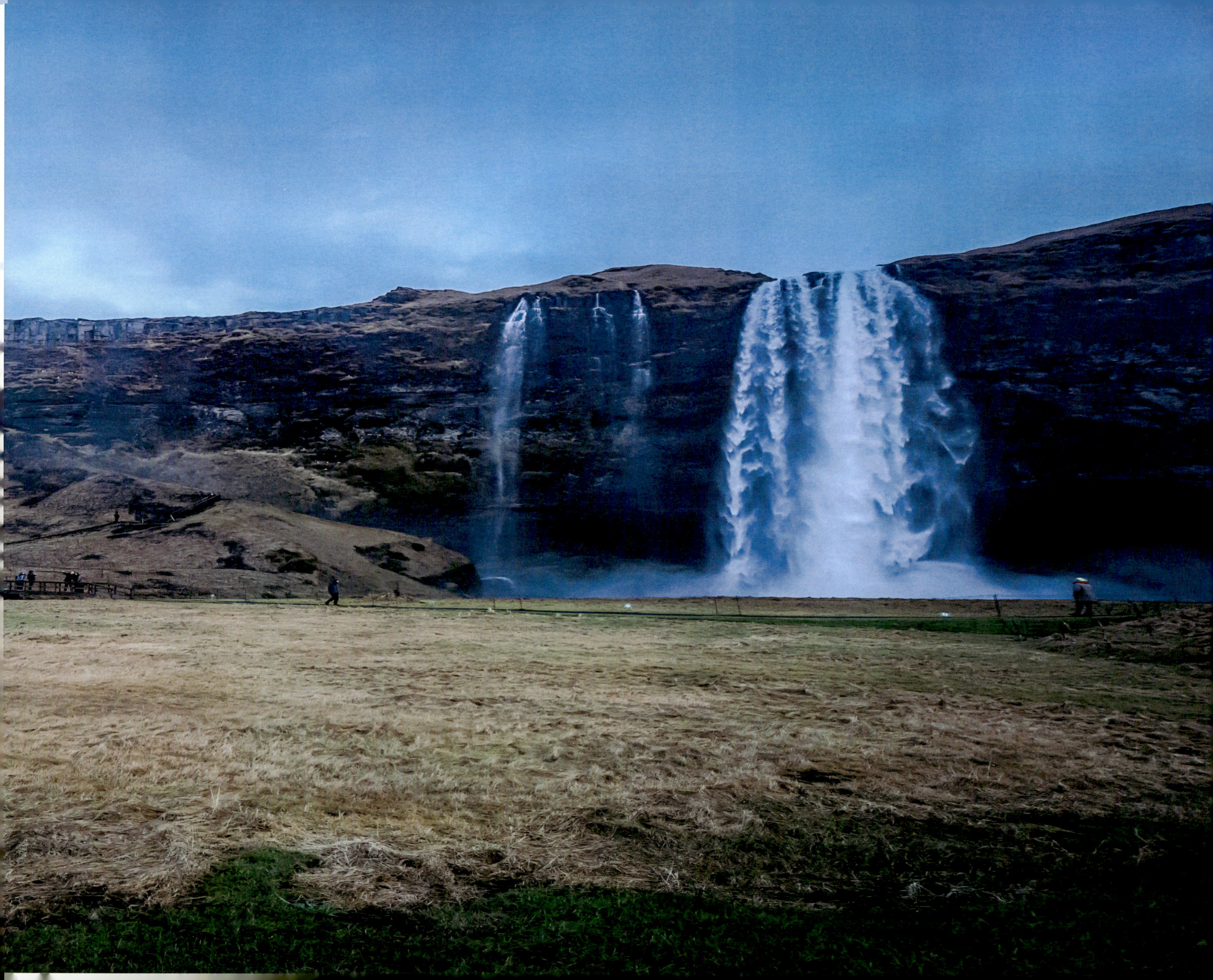

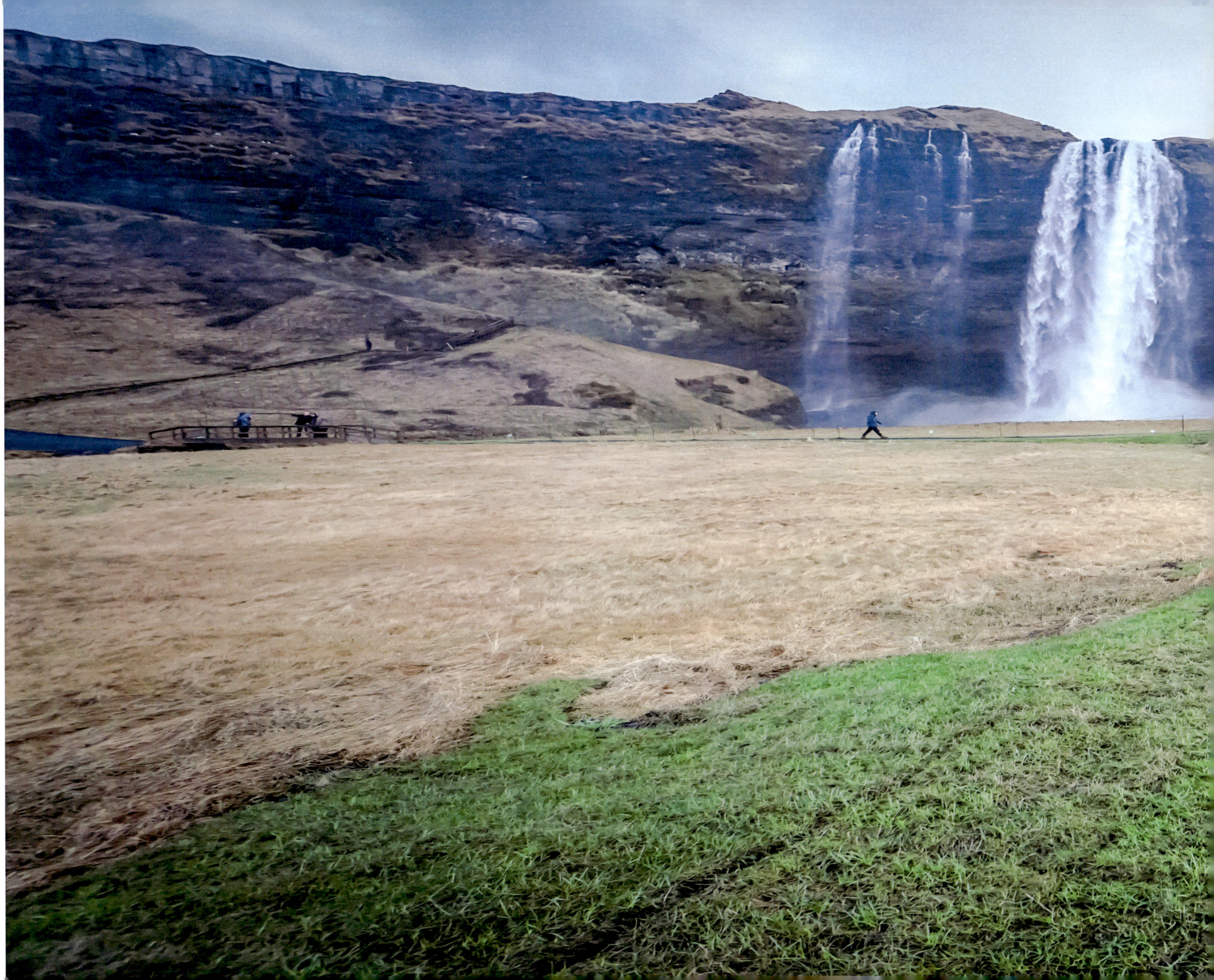

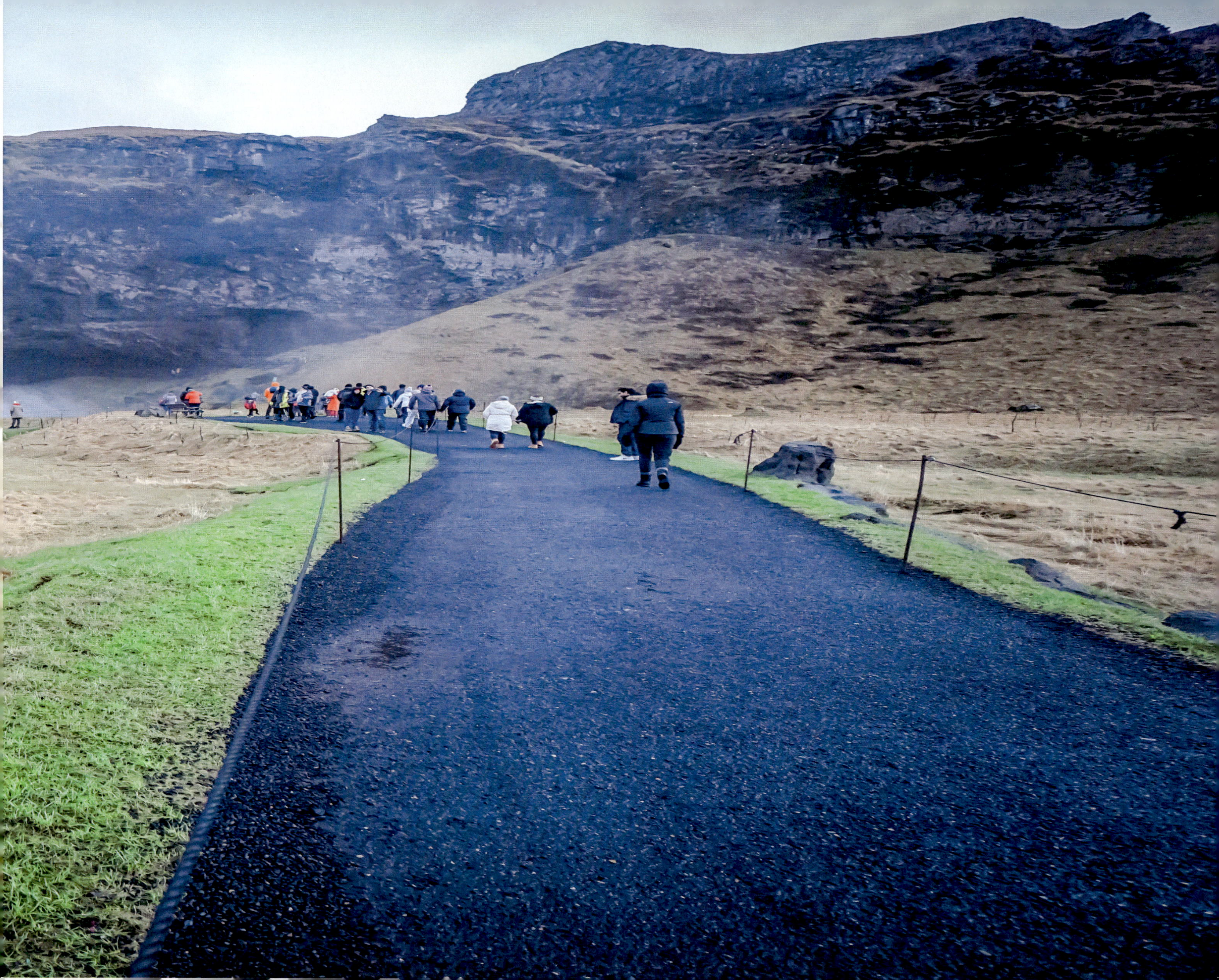

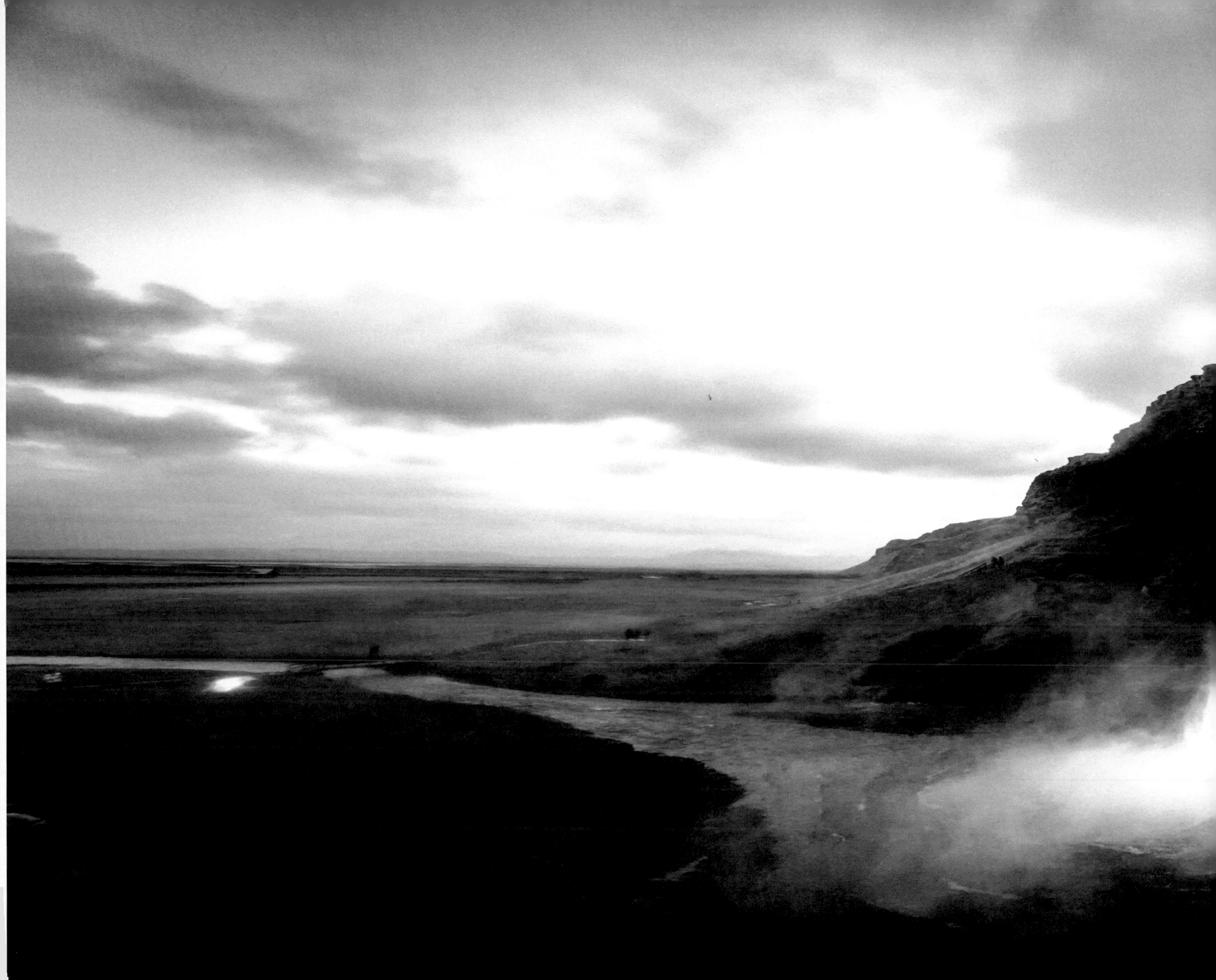

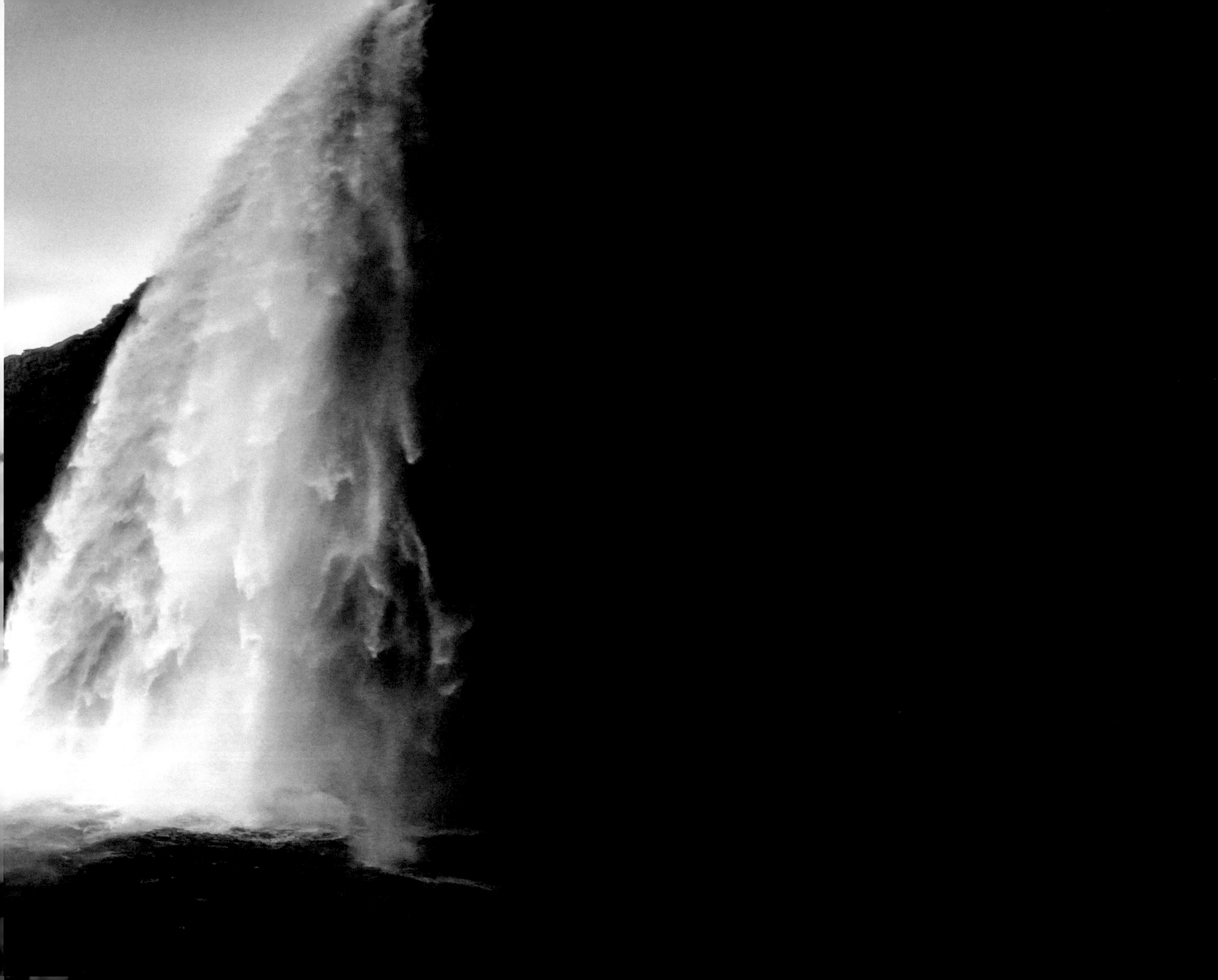

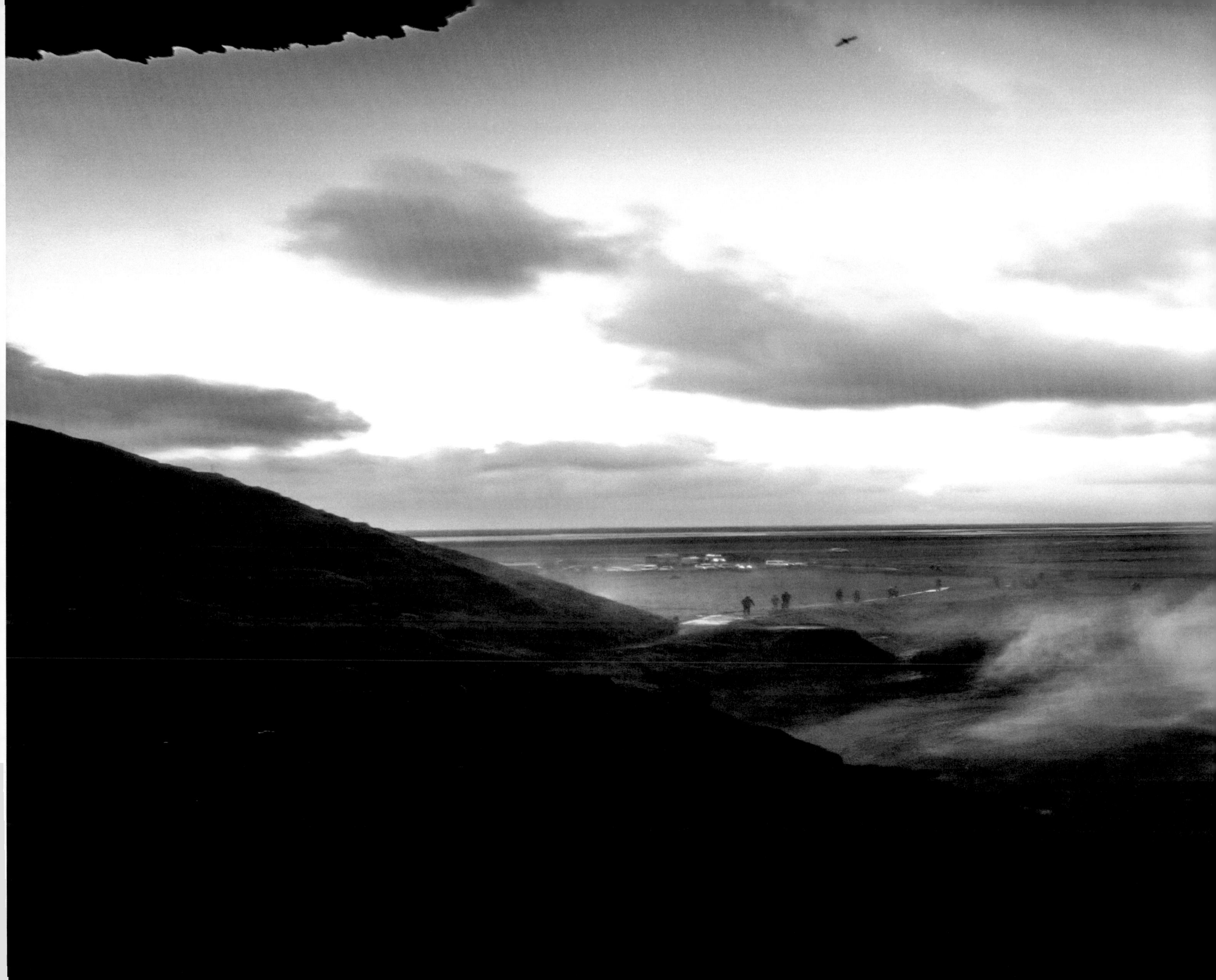

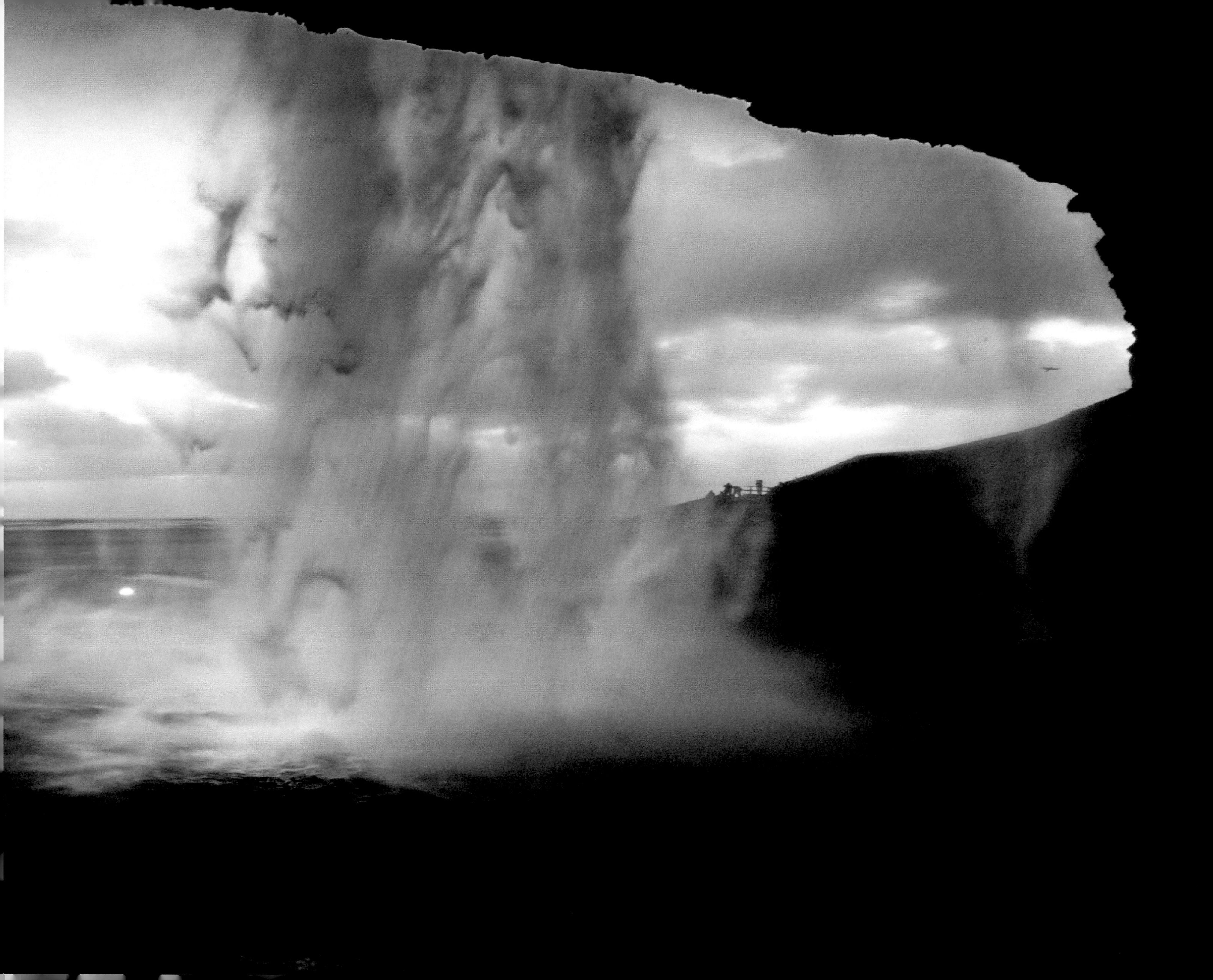

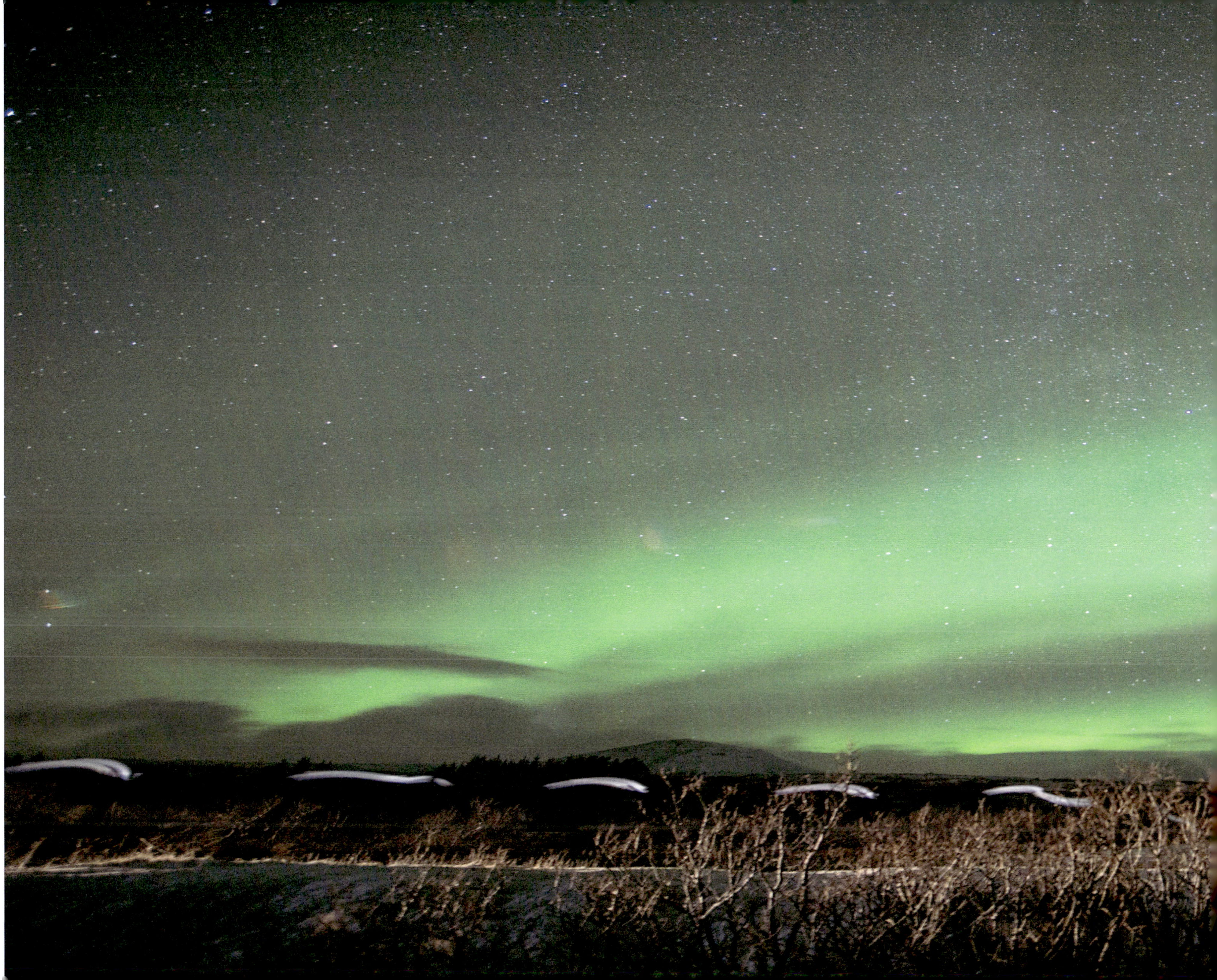

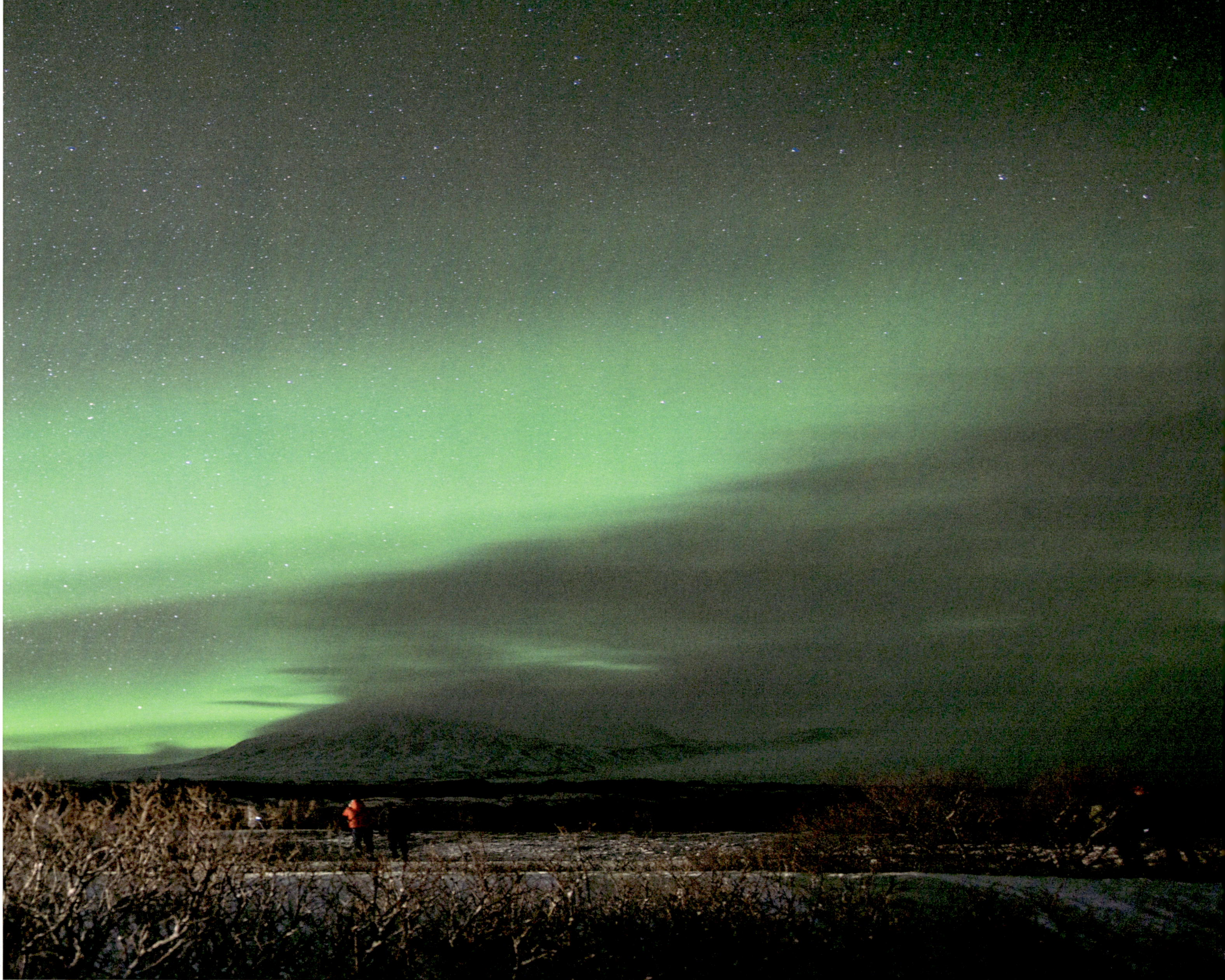

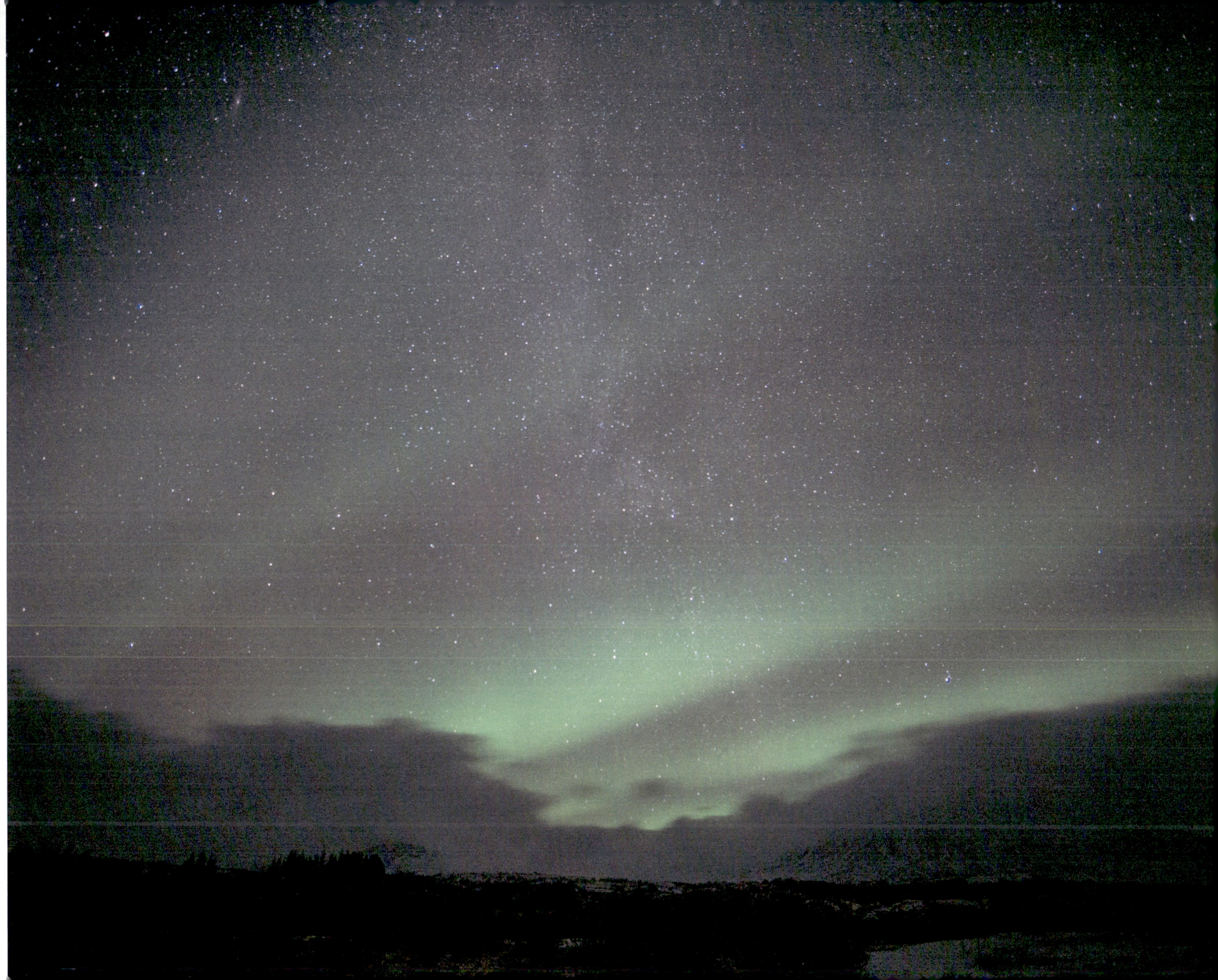

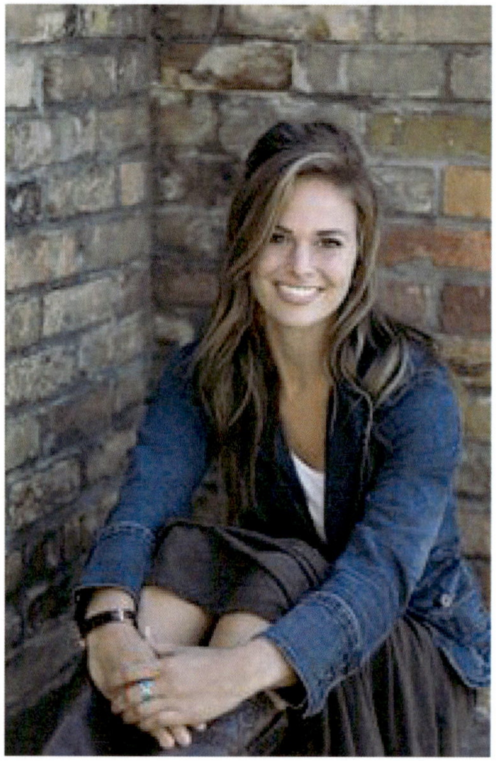

Social Media & Contact

www.shutter-fotos.ca

elyse@shutter-fotos.ca

@shutter_fotos

@ShutterFotos

@FotoBoothphotography

About the Author

Elyse Booth is an international photographer and educator. She has travelled around the world photographing nature, people, culture, architectural icons, animals and lifestyle content. A few of the places she has travelled to include: Hawaii, Iceland, Thailand, Cambodia, Malaysia, Laos, Italy, France, Ireland, Croatia, Hungary, Czech Republic, England, Scotland, Costa Rica, Bermuda and Mexico.

Elyse is an award winning Google trusted photographer. She builds virtual tours for Google Maps through her business Shutter Fotos, www.shutter-fotos.ca. Elyse has been recognized as a top performer for Google and top five in North America for her tours.

Elyse has a passion for lifelong learning. In addition to her love for travel and photography, she teaches Communications Technology in the private and public educational systems.

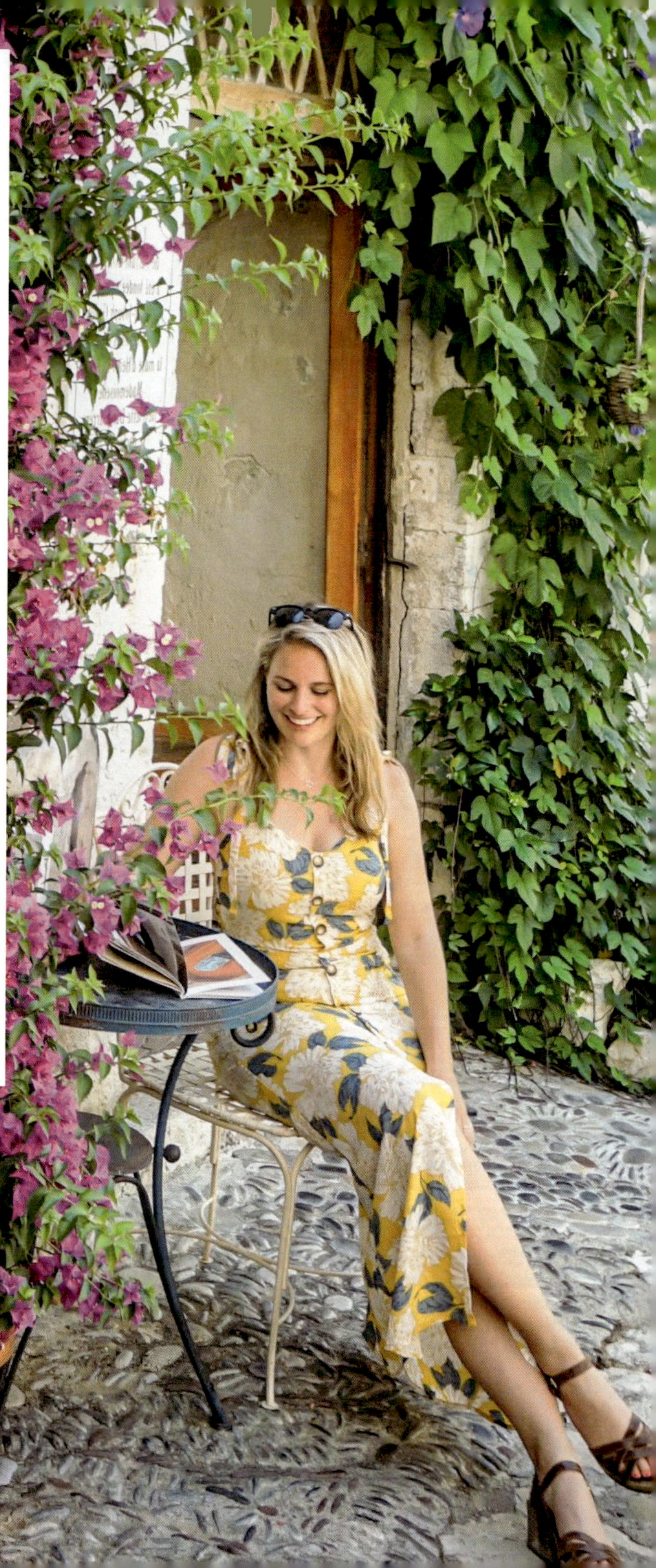

www.ingramcontent.com/pod-product-compliance
Ingram Content Group UK Ltd.
Pitfield, Milton Keynes, MK11 3LW, UK
UKRC031108040826
14089UKWH00040B/243

* 9 7 8 1 7 7 7 0 6 2 1 6 3 *